Essential London

by

SUSAN GROSSMAN

Susan Grossman is a travel writer, broadcaster and
photographer, and is a former travel editor of the
London Telegraph Sunday Magazine.
She has presented two series of the BBC's
'Food and Drink' programme.

Little, Brown and Company
Boston   Toronto   London

REVISED EDITION

The contents of this publication are believed correct at the time of printing.
Nevertheless, the publishers cannot accept responsibility for errors or
omissions, nor for changes in details given. We are always grateful to readers
who let us know of any errors or omissions they come across, and future
printings will be updated accordingly.

Produced by the Publishing Division of The Automobile Association of Great
Britain.

Written by Susan Grossman
"Peace and Quiet" section by Paul Sterry
Consultant: Frank Dawes

ISBN 0-316-25027-9

10 9 8 7 6 5 4 3 2 1

PRINTED IN TRENTO, ITALY

This book employs a
simple rating system to
help choose which
places to visit:

◆◆◆   do not miss

◆◆   see if you can

◆   worth seeing if
      you have time

INTRODUCTION

Although London is changing rapidly, with new things to see and do appearing by the day, it is still a city with a profound and lively sense of history. This guide's aim is to provide the sort of information a Londoner would give to a friend visiting the capital. In it you will find everything from the newest museums to a personal selection of shops, hotels and restaurants. What you won't find is information on where to have an Elizabethan banquet; neither are there pages and pages of historical facts. This book does set out to show you a side of the British capital usually reserved for residents!

Present-day London

London has some 24 million visitors each year, over three times its population. For most, first impressions are not particularly inspiring, whether your approach is by train through the dreary south London suburbs from Gatwick, by coach from Heathrow in the west, or by subway into Piccadilly. Once in the city you may be shocked by the crowds, the traffic, the down-and-outs and the homeless teenagers asking for money at the foot of the escalators on the Underground, as the subway is called. As for the litter, every year a pile of garbage big enough to fill Trafalgar Square to five times the height of Nelson's Column is swept up.

Enough of the negatives. Get your bearings and you will discover a city with more green spaces than most, with enough culture to fill a filofax; culinary offerings that span the globe and an exciting future as whole areas of the capital are redeveloped.

London looks its best on a Sunday when the streets are relatively quiet (so long as plans for Sunday shop opening don't go ahead) and the office workers are at home eating roast beef and Yorkshire pudding after a quick pint in the pub. It looks its best in spring or early summer with the crocuses and daffodils carpeting the parks. And it looks pretty good too at night, especially from Waterloo Bridge, with the main monuments lit up along the Embankment.

Open spaces are an essential part of London's character. They vary from parks so big as to be almost open countryside, to squares little bigger than suburban gardens. This is St James's Square

Symbol of democracy. The Palace of Westminster (universally known as the Houses of Parliament) was rebuilt in the years after 1834, when its predecessor was burnt down. The Victoria Tower dominates this view, with 'Big Ben' looking small in the distance, an illusion which emphasises the huge size of the palace

Old London

Julius Caesar invaded Britain in 55BC, but it took another 100 years for his legions to land on the south coast and transform the site into a major town. It was Edward the Confessor who moved upstream from the City to establish Westminster, rebuilding the Abbey and the Royal Palace. The City retaliated by electing its own mayor; and it also established itself as the centre for trade, which it still is.

Monarchs came and went. The Black Death of 1348 did not stop the expansion and by the time Henry VIII came to power in 1509 London's population was 50,000. Henry, now famous for having had six wives, sparked off centuries of religious conflict when, in order to divorce his first wife and marry Anne Boleyn, he led the country in a break away from Papal authority. Under the rule of Henry and Anne's daughter,

Elizabeth I, London enjoyed a flourishing of
literature and theatre: this was the age of
Shakespeare and of the city's first theatre, the
Globe, built in 1599. This was also a time of
increasing debate between Parliament and
monarch over the balance of political power.
The 17th century brought civil war, when
Parliament challenged Charles I's use of royal
authority and his toleration of Catholicism. After
the victory of Parliamentarian forces, led by
Oliver Cromwell, the King was executed and a
period of strict Puritan government ensued. The
monarchy was restored in 1660, when Charles II
ushered in a period of stability, earning the title
of 'Merry Monarch'.

In 1665 yet another plague hit the capital, and a
year later, a small fire in Pudding Lane triggered
off flames that fed the Great Fire of London which
destroyed four-fifths of the city. Rebuilding was

INTRODUCTION

soon under way, and for the next few centuries London prospered. But many of the inhabitants lived in squalor, and crime was rife.

By the 19th century London had expanded enormously, but pockets of the capital were trapped in harsh poverty, vividly described in Charles Dickens' novels.

The first railway appeared during Queen Victoria's reign, as did the first Underground or 'tube' line, which first carried passengers in 1890. From then on suburbs began to spread alongside the railway tracks.

Government

London is the seat of British government, which is a constitutional monarchy. Its laws are made in Parliament, which has two 'Houses', both at Westminster: the House of Commons, to which Members are elected; and the House of Lords, which can delay and amend laws but can no longer veto them altogether. The House of Lords,

People! On an average day in London you can see bowler-hatted businessmen and penniless paupers, frantically rich yuppies and blue-bloods from the country, the genuinely eccentric and the desperately comic

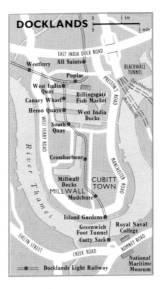

denounced by some as unrepresentative and anachronistic, was once a powerful centre of patronage, and the creation of peers to add weight to one political party carried on well into this century. Britain has no written constitution – another subject of lively debate. Its form of government evolved through centuries of power struggles between nobles, parliaments and monarchs. In theory, the monarch can still veto the country's laws, and the Queen must still ratify all statutes. But in practice this is now a formality which, like the approval of a new Prime Minister by 'kissing hands', has become one of the city's political rituals.

New London

They're calling it the largest building site in the world as the biggest building boom London has seen in 25 years gets underway. But unless you base your visit in among the cranes of London's Docklands or in among the banks of the City, you would hardly know that some 20 million square ft (1,800,000 sq m) of new office space has already been approved.

Not all Londoners are happy about what's

happening to their city, least of all Prince
Charles, who has complained that post-war
architectural clutter has already obscured some
of the famous 'views'. Rather late in the day, the
Government has now agreed that views along
the river and around the Palace of Westminster
should be protected. The answer seems to lie in
'groundscrapers', a sort of tower block turned on
its side, and they are mushrooming up.
To the east of the city centre, Docklands is
already undergoing an enormous change as the
old warehouses of the West India Dock are
transformed into luxury office buildings and
apartments. Of more interest to the visitor are
the London Arena entertainment complex at

Limeharbour and the vast shopping centre at
Wapping's Tobacco Dock. There is just one
thing that might hinder Docklands' meteoric rise
in status, and that's communications. There isn't
adequate public transport and road links are
poor. Within the next few years a massive one-
third of the part of London known as the City will
be redeveloped in order to place it firmly on the
'global digital highway'. Many of the buildings
will be offices, but entertainment and culture
have not been forgotten. The Broadgate site of
ultra-modern offices already has at its centre, a
small open-air skating rink, while at Butler's
Wharf, on the south bank of the Thames near
Tower Bridge, there is a new Conran Foundation

*St Katharine's
Dock. Originally
built in the 1820s,
the warehouses
here stored wool
and wine. They
eventually closed
in 1968, victims to
new downriver
ports. Today the
expensive boats
give a clue to the
'new money' that
has transformed
them*

*Nautical whimsy at
Hays Galleria*

Design Museum, and 19th-century warehouses
are being turned into shops. The thriving London
Bridge City complex includes the impressive
glass-domed Hays Galleria shopping centre
overlooking the Thames (good views here of the
huge Royal Navy cruiser HMS *Belfast*), and by
1993 there will be a re-construction of
Shakespeare's Globe Theatre on the Thames
opposite St Paul's.

Buildings that went up in the 1960s elsewhere in
London are being demolished or getting a
facelift. The South Bank (Hayward Gallery,
Queen Elizabeth Hall and Royal Festival Hall)
and the ugly concrete high-level walkways
linking them are due to get a massive multi-
million dollar camouflage. A similarly large
amount of money has been spent on turning the
old Battersea Power Station, into a mammoth
shopping and leisure centre, but plans have
faltered and its future is uncertain. Whether or
not all these changes will enhance London's
already rather haphazard appearance, only time
will tell.

THE DIFFERENT AREAS

London is split into different areas, each with a distinctive character of its own, from the centre of commerce – the City – to the political world of Westminster. When you are trying to locate an address, the postal code can provide useful information. Places in west, west central and southwest London have W, WC and SW respectively after their address, followed by a low number if they are central locations. Addresses with east (E) and east central (EC) after them are in the City, while northwest London (NW) includes areas like Hampstead. The higher the number, the further into the suburbs the location is. London is divided by the River Thames, and most of the action takes place north of it. Stay anywhere in the West End, Knightsbridge, Bayswater or Victoria and you will easily be able to reach the main shopping areas and places of interest.

Inner London
Bayswater
Part of Paddington, near Marble Arch and Hyde Park, are full of hotels. The busy Bayswater Road runs past Notting Hill (home of the famous carnival and Portobello Road antique market) and Holland Park to Shepherd's Bush in one direction and along to Marble Arch and Oxford Street in the other. The surrounding streets are quiet, and full of family homes and embassies. Knightsbridge is situated on the other side of Hyde Park.

Hyde Park Corner can be one of London's most unpleasant traffic bottlenecks, but these horses seem quite at home

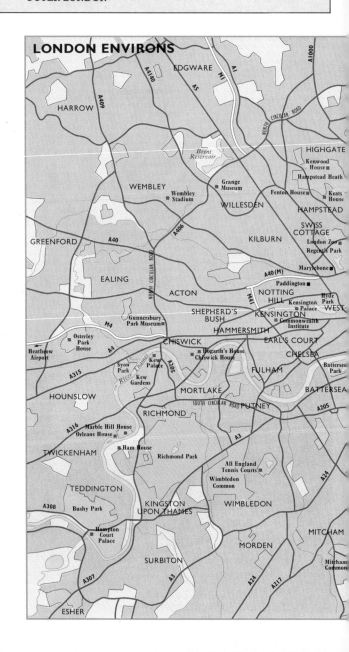

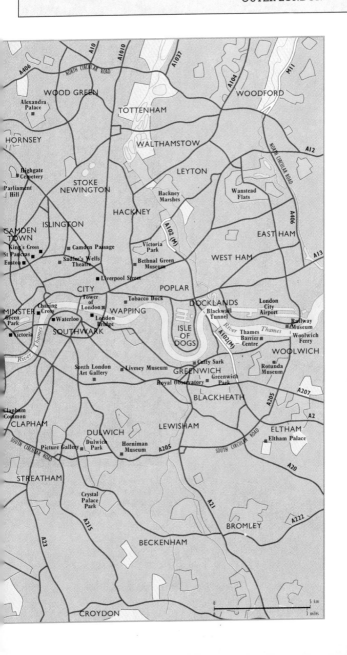

THE DIFFERENT AREAS

Bloomsbury

Bloomsbury is behind New Oxford Street and Tottenham Court Road (with its electronics and furniture shops). It includes quiet squares, the British Museum, the University of London and University College Hospital. Famous residents in the 1920s and 30s were Virginia Woolf, E M Forster, Rupert Brooke, D H Lawrence and Bertrand Russell, all members of the intellectual circle of friends, the 'Bloomsbury Group'.

Chelsea

Chelsea has upmarket residential properties, many of them small terraced houses in quiet squares, with fashionable addresses like Cheyne Walk on the river. The new Chelsea Harbour development of restaurants, offices and expensive riverside apartments overlooks the boats. The King's Road, the 'mecca' in the 1960s, is still one of London's fashion streets. Chelsea is a tube or bus ride from the West End's shops and theatres, a short way from Knightsbridge, and it runs into Kensington.

The City

The City is both the historic capital and the centre of commerce, with boundaries that have extended west into Holborn and east into Docklands. It is a hive of activity during the week as brokers do business on the foreign exchanges, nipping out to one of the many historic hostelries for lunch.

On weekends it is relatively quiet, as the owners of the pin-stripe suits and the occasional

The nave of St Paul's. The monument on the left is the overwhelming memorial to the Duke of Wellington, who was buried in the crypt

bowler hat desert the old Square Mile and head south of the river to the Stockbroker Belt. The younger 'yuppies' with their Porsches relax in apartments in Fulham, the Docklands or the Barbican. Meanwhile, the

cockney heart (cockneys are Londoners born within the sound of Bow Bells) still throbs among the barrows in the East End markets, the historic centre still lives in the ancient Livery Halls, and the wigged barristers still administer justice in the peace and inner sanctum of The Temple. The skyline is ever changing, though familiar landmarks like St Paul's Cathedral, the Bank of England and the Old Bailey are still distinguishable through the cranes. It is an area rich in things to see, including 39 city churches and the Museum of London. Close by though not strictly in the City, are the Tower of London, HMS *Belfast*, Tower Bridge, and the Hays Galleria shopping centre, in the London Bridge City Complex.

THE DIFFERENT AREAS

Covent Garden

A compact central area, next to Soho, immortalised in Shaw's *Pygmalion* where the young Eliza Doolittle sold flowers to the ladies and gents emerging from the Royal Opera House. The Opera House is still there, but the vegetable and flower market moved out in 1974. Today Covent Garden is a magnet for visitors, who throng the cobbled piazza to shop in the central market (idiosyncratic shops selling everything from doll's houses to flower perfumes) and watch the free live street entertainment. On weekends there are crafts and antiques sold from the original wrought-iron trading stands. During the week the open-air cafés, restaurants and wine bars, though few of high quality, are full of film and advertising executives from the surrounding offices. Attractions in the area include the London Transport Museum and several theatres, but there are relatively few hotels.

Covent Garden is an essential destination for many shoppers and other visitors

Docklands

Before World War II, London was the greatest port in the world, and 120,000 dockers handled cargoes of spices, furs, rubber and sugar. By the early 1960s the Docks were in irreversible decline and by 1982 everything had closed. Recently, some £2 billion has been invested in the area; Canary Wharf is set to become the new financial centre and 600 companies have already moved in, although it will be some time before the cranes and bulldozers move out. The Docklands Light Railway, the London City Airport and some 12,000 new homes are already installed, as is the huge shopping centre at Tobacco Dock. The best way to see what's happening to Docklands is to travel on the Docklands Light Railway (weekdays only) from Tower Gateway (Bank from summer 1991) near the Tower of London to Island Gardens on the Isle of Dogs. You can then take the old dockers' foot tunnel ('subway') under the Thames across to Greenwich.

Fulham

A mix of seedy tenement houses and fashionable squares. Parts of Fulham are on the river. The Knightsbridge end is upmarket with a good range of restaurants and shopping. Much of the rest is pretty nondescript. Fulham runs into neighbouring Chelsea.

Kensington

The High Street is now largely occupied by chain stores, but this Royal Borough still has its exclusive parts from the antique shops in Kensington Church Street to Kensington Palace and the surrounding gardens. Holland Park and the Commonwealth Institute are also in Kensington (see also South Kensington and Earl's Court, page 21).

Knightsbridge

A very central, exclusive location with some of the more expensive hotels and residences in quiet squares. Home of Harrods, Harvey Nichols, Bonham's auctioneers, quality fashion shops in Sloane Street and Knightsbridge, plus numerous galleries and antique shops. Opposite Hyde Park.

Mayfair and Park Lane

High rents render Mayfair, which includes the West End (see page 22), Bond Street and Park Lane, one of the most exclusive areas in London. Famous hotels line one side of Park Lane and overlook Hyde Park, and other well-known hotels like Claridges and the Connaught are nearby. Mayfair's village heart is Shepherd Market (home to high-class prostitutes). The area has famous squares like Berkeley and Grosvenor (home of the American Embassy), and includes Bond Street and the *haute couture* fashion houses, as well as Curzon Street's gambling houses. Attractions include the Museum of Mankind, near the Burlington Arcade, the Royal Academy in Burlington House, and, just outside the area, in Manchester Square, the Wallace Collection, with its 18th-century paintings and French furniture.

THE DIFFERENT AREAS

Piccadilly and St James's

Piccadilly is a busy thoroughfare connecting Hyde Park and Leicester Square. Green Park runs along one side of it. Within Piccadilly you will find the Ritz Hotel, the Burlington Arcade, the Royal Academy, Fortnum and Mason and airline offices. St James's, to the south, is a largely male-orientated area with tailors in Jermyn Street, and several gentlemen's clubs. There are theatres in the Haymarket.

Regent's Park

Nash's beautiful terraces dominate the architecture of Regent's Park, behind the busy Marylebone Road (Madame Tussaud's and the Planetarium) and Baker Street. Attractions include Queen Mary's Rose Garden, in full bloom in June, the open-air theatre and the Zoo. The Regent's Canal leads to Camden Lock, with its weekend market, and Little Venice (Maida Vale).

Soho

Soho runs into Covent Garden. Once London's red-light district, Soho has cleaned up its act. Most of the sleazy nightclubs have shut and been replaced by designer restaurants and shops (although the famous Raymond Revuebar Theatre is still going strong). A handful of family-owned businesses still thrive in the area, including Continental delicatessens and patisseries. The Berwick Street market dates back to 1778. One of the few areas of London alive after midnight, with trendy bars, brasseries and discos, Soho includes the cinemas in Leicester Square, the Trocadero

'Little Venice' – the prettiest stretch of the Regent's Canal

Centre (shops and entertainment), the bookshops in Charing Cross Road and cinemas and theatres in Shaftesbury Avenue. Chinatown, south of Shaftesbury Avenue, is also part of Soho.

South Bank

The South Bank Arts Centre across Waterloo Bridge, overlooking the Thames, has for years been the most important landmark for visitors south of the

to stay in if you're attending an exhibition at Earl's Court or Olympia and near to the main museums (Victoria and Albert, Science, Natural History and Geological) and public transport, but some way from theatres and the West End. It is full of reasonably priced small hotels and guesthouses, though you might find the neighbourhood a bit scruffy. Hotels in or around Kensington High Street are nearer the exclusive shops.

The Strand, Charing Cross

The Strand runs from Trafalgar Square, past Charing Cross Station (with its new rooftop 'groundscraper') to the Aldwych which adjoins Fleet Street. To the north is Covent Garden, to the south the river. The Strand's most famous landmark is the Savoy Hotel, and the street contains several theatres. At the Aldwych end are Bush House, the BBC's World Service headquarters, and Somerset House, which now houses the Courtauld Institute Galleries. If you listen to the bells at St Clement Danes Church (on weekdays at 9:00A.M., noon, 3:00P.M. or 6:00P.M.) you will hear the famous 'Oranges and Lemons' nursery rhyme. London's journalists have largely moved out of Fleet Street to Wapping and the Isle of Dogs, but the barristers are still at the Temple and in the four Inns of Court, a series of secluded cobbled courtyards (you can wander around the quadrangles) seemingly divorced from the bustle of the rest of London. The Royal Courts of Justice occupy an impressive cathedral-like building in the Strand.

river. It includes the Royal Festival Hall, the National Theatre, the Queen Elizabeth Hall, the Hayward Gallery, the National Film Theatre and the Museum of the Moving Image, all due for a £200 million facelift. New developments (mostly offices and possibly a hotel) may well change the skyline.

South Kensington and Earl's Court

This part of west London is a lively cosmopolitan area, useful

THE DIFFERENT AREAS

Victoria
Numerous small hotels cater to new arrivals whose first view of London is the Station. Busy Victoria Street leads to the Palace of Westminster. Buckingham Palace is to the north, Knightsbridge to the west. The area is fairly quiet at night.

West End
The West End is part of Mayfair and Soho, a large area that takes in the shops and department stores in Oxford Street and Regent Street and the theatres around Leicester Square and Covent Garden. North of Oxford Street, Harley Street and Wigmore Street are full of dentists' and doctors' consulting rooms.

Westminster
Seat of Royalty (Buckingham Palace) and Government, Westminster has the Houses of Parliament and Big Ben, Westminster Abbey, Westminster Cathedral, Whitehall (with its Government buildings) and Horse Guards Parade leading up to Trafalgar Square. The area is near the river with good public transport to other parts of the capital. Other sights include the Tate Gallery. A relatively quiet area, especially in the evenings.

Outer London – North
Camden Town
A cosmopolitan residential area somewhat dominated by the crowds who descend on weekends to visit Camden Lock market (crafts, jewellery) or to take a boat trip on the Regent's Canal. A short ride by tube into central London. Good shopping for prints, pine furniture and

Buckingham Palace and the Queen Victoria Memorial

books (with many shops open on Sundays). Restaurants (brasseries and Greek) and wine bars. TV AM television studios, London Zoo, Regent's Park, Little Venice and Hampstead are nearby.

Hampstead
On the Northern Line tube into town. Village atmosphere with apartments and houses occupied by writers, professionals and bohemians. Narrow pretty streets up behind the station, lots of pubs, restaurants and boutiques and, at the top of the hill, the

wide open spaces of Hampstead Heath. Join the Sunday afternoon kite flyers on Parliament Hill for fine views of the capital. In summer you can swim in the ponds, or watch an open-air concert, while picnicking in the grounds of Kenwood House.

Other Northern Suburbs

Swiss Cottage, down the road from Hampstead, has numerous cosmopolitan restaurants in the Finchley Road, and good shopping. Lords, in **St John's Wood**, a short bus ride from Baker Street and near Regent's Park, will be familiar to cricket fans. Further north is **Highgate** (Karl Marx is buried in the cemetery) and **Islington**, which has a good antique market (Camden Passage) as well as the Sadler's Wells Theatre.

Outer London – South

It is more difficult to get into central London by public transport from most places south of the river than it is from those north.

Greenwich

Directly across the river from Docklands and the Isle of Dogs via the foot tunnel under the Thames, built in 1897 for dockworkers of the West India Docks. Things to see include the *Cutty Sark* and the Old Royal Observatory (home of the Greenwich Meridian). River boats from Greenwich continue along the river to Westminster.

Richmond

Lies between Hampton Court (see What to See, page 25) and Hammersmith Bridge. The best

way to get there is by boat (summer only) from Westminster Pier. Richmond also encompasses Mortlake, Twickenham, Ham, Barnes, Teddington and Kew (with its magnificent Royal Botanic Gardens). You can walk along the river or stroll or ride through the 2,500 acres of Richmond Park where you may or may not catch sight of deer.

Richmond Park is just like 'real' countryside except that the deer don't run away!

Other Southern Suburbs

Dulwich and **Blackheath** are affluent residential areas.

WHAT TO SEE

Museums, Exhibitions and Galleries

Among the most popular sights in London are the British Museum, the National Gallery, the Science Museum, Madame Tussaud's, the Tower of London (see page 42) and the Tate Gallery. Three of the major museums, the Science, Natural History and Victoria and Albert, are next to each other in South Kensington (not far from Harrods), although they are so large you may not find it possible to 'do' more than one or two at a time, and it may be best to stick to one section and 'do' it thoroughly.

Many museums are shut on some, but not necessarily all, public holidays. Most charge admission. Exceptions are indicated in the lists below and include the British Museum, the Museum of London, the Tate Gallery and the National Gallery. Children and Senior Citizens usually pay less and under 5's nothing. Below is a selection out of the hundreds of museums in and around the capital.

Central London

♦
BANK OF ENGLAND MUSEUM
Bartholomew Lane, EC2
Opened at the end of 1988, this museum tells the story of the 300 years of history of the 'Old Lady of Threadneedle Street', with an exhibition that includes gold bars, banknotes and a video. Free.
Open: Monday to Friday 10:00A.M. to 5:00P.M.; also summer weekends 11:00A.M. to 5:00P.M.
Tube: Bank

♦♦♦
BRITISH MUSEUM
Great Russell Street, WC1
One of the biggest and best museums in the world with numerous treasures grouped by date and nationality. Prehistoric Britain, Egyptian mummies, Islamic art, and Greek and Roman antiquities are just a few of the subjects covered. Don't miss the Magna Carta, the Sutton Hoo treasure or the Elgin Marbles. The ethnography collection is in the Museum of Mankind in Burlington Gardens. Shop, café and restaurant. Free.
Open: Monday to Saturday 10:00A.M. to 5:00P.M., Sunday 2:30P.M. to 6:00P.M.
Tube: Russell Square, Holborn, Tottenham Court Road

♦♦
COURTAULD INSTITUTE GALLERIES
North Block, Somerset House, Strand, WC2
Some of the most exciting French paintings in London are here – with work by Monet, Bonnard, Degas, Seurat and Cézanne. There is also a fine collection of Old Masters. Bookshop and café.
Open: Monday to Saturday 10:00A.M. to 5:00P.M., Sunday 2:00P.M. to 6:00P.M.
Tube: Aldwych, Temple

♦
DESIGN MUSEUM
Butlers Wharf, 28 Shad Thames, SE1
Opened summer 1989. Exhibitions of design and graphics in a modern white building converted from a 1950s warehouse. Run by the Conran Foundation and partly

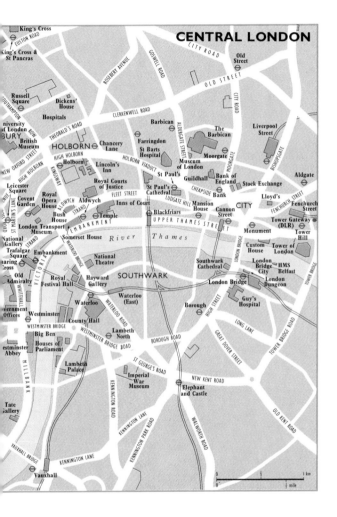

CENTRAL LONDON

WHAT TO SEE

modelled on the Boilerhouse
which they leased out in the
basement of the Victoria and
Albert Museum until 1986.
Open: Tuesday to Sunday
11:30A.M. to 6:30P.M.; closed
Mondays.
Tube: Tower Hill or London
Bridge (or Design Museum
riverboat from Tower Pier to
Butlers Wharf Pier)

◆
FLORENCE NIGHTINGALE MUSEUM
2 Lambeth Palace Road, SE1
A small museum dedicated to
the life of the Lady of the Lamp,
opened early 1989 next to St
Thomas's Hospital where she
founded the first School of
Nursing in 1860. Unique
collection of memorabilia
including the medicine chest
and lamp she used during the
Crimean War.
Open: Tuesday to Sunday
10:00A.M. to 4:00P.M.; closed
Mondays
Tube: Waterloo, Westminster

◆
GEOLOGICAL MUSEUM
(now part of Natural History
Museum) *Exhibition Road, SW7*
Gem stones, rocks and fossils
plus an earthquake simulator
and video of a volcano, part of
'The Story of the Earth'. Other
special exhibits include 'Britain
before Man', 'Treasures of
the Earth', 'Gem Stones' and
'Britain's Offshore Oil and Gas'.
Combined ticket with Natural
History Museum and linkway
through. Activities for families.
Open: Monday to Saturday
10:00A.M. to 6:00P.M.; Sunday
1:00P.M. to 6:00P.M.
Free admission 4:30P.M. to 6:00P.M.

(Monday to Friday), 5:00P.M. to
6:00P.M. (weekends)
Tube: South Kensington

◆
GUINNESS WORLD OF RECORDS
*The Trocadero, Coventry Street,
Piccadilly, W1*
The first exhibition organised by
Guinness. The displays illustrate
feats from the *Guinness Book of
Records*, one of the world's best-
selling books. Fun for anyone
interested in world records, this
is a colourful exhibition of feats
and achievements from the tallest
man to the fastest runner. Push-
buttons and scale models.
Open: 10:00A.M. to 10:00P.M. daily
Tube: Piccadilly Circus,
Leicester Square

◆
HAYWARD GALLERY
*South Bank Centre, Waterloo,
SE1*
Housed in a specially-built,
modern building, opened in
1968. On the South Bank (next to
the National Theatre and the
Festival Hall), with changing art
exhibitions. The gallery's
exhibitions concentrate on 20th-
century work.
Open: Monday to Wednesday
10:00A.M. to 8:00P.M., Thursday to
Saturday 10:00A.M. to 6:00P.M.,
Sunday noon to 6:00P.M.
Tube: Waterloo, Embankment

◆◆
IMPERIAL WAR MUSEUM
Lambeth Road, SE1
Newly redesigned museum, with
exhibits never previously
displayed. Story of war in our
century in a triple height
exhibition hall with exhibits
including aircraft, tanks, Polaris

Quiet recreation – inside London Brass Rubbing Centre

missiles and torpedoes. The building which houses the museum, formerly the original 'Bedlam', Bethlehem Royal Hospital (a lunatic asylum), has been revamped and adapted to include such features as an enormous glazed atrium. Aircraft seem to fly around the room and visitors can roam freely among the displays. Various themes including the 'Blitz and Trench Experiences' and the 'Post-War World'. Free Fridays.
Open: daily 10:00A.M. to 6:00P.M.
Tube: Lambeth North, Elephant and Castle

◆
LONDON BRASS RUBBING CENTRE
St Martin-in-the-Fields Church, Trafalgar Square, WC2
Brass rub to medieval music. Some 70 replica church brasses

to choose from – charge. (Note: You can also rub brasses at Westminster Abbey – Monday to Saturday 9:00A.M. to 5:00P.M.)
Open: Monday to Saturday 9:00A.M. to 5:00P.M.
Tube: Charing Cross, Leicester Square

◆
LONDON DUNGEON
28–34 Tooley Street, SE1
Opposite Hays Galleria and near HMS *Belfast*. Gruesome, dimly lit exhibition of medieval history including the Plague, the Great Fire of London, astrology and witchcraft. Lots of torture and gore with appropriate noises. Life-size reconstruction of Pudding Lane, where the Great Fire began. No under 10's on their own.
Open: April to September 10:00A.M. to 6:30P.M. (to 5:30P.M. rest of the year)
Tube: London Bridge

WHAT TO SEE

◆◆
LONDON TRANSPORT MUSEUM
Covent Garden, WC2
All sorts of transport from trolley buses to trains housed in the old Flower Market building in the Covent Garden piazza. Lots of things to scramble over, and you can work signals on trains or 'drive' a bus or a tube train. Special events for children and families during school vacations.
Open: all year except Christmas, 10:00A.M. to 6:00P.M.
Tube: Covent Garden

◆◆
MADAME TUSSAUD'S
Marylebone Road, NW1
One of the most popular attractions in London, with life-like wax figures (continuously updated) of famous people from historical figures to pop stars. Plus the Chamber of Horrors, which includes reconstructions of some grisly and historic crimes. Combined ticket with the Planetarium (see separate entry) next door. Expect long lines.
Open: daily 10:00A.M. to 5:30P.M. Doors open half an hour earlier on weekends and one hour earlier during July and August.
Tube: Baker Street

◆◆
MUSEUM OF LONDON
150 London Wall, EC2
The museum to visit if you are interested in the history of London and Londoners. Open-plan galleries of well-displayed exhibits from pre-historic cave men to an elevator from Selfridges department store. Also the Lord Mayor's State Coach, reconstructed Victorian shops, a 1930's Ford motorcar, an air-raid shelter and a reconstruction of Newgate prison. One of the highlights is a re-enactment of the Fire of London. Features of special interest include the superb models of William the Conqueror's White Tower and old St Paul's. Café. Free.
Open: Tuesday to Saturday 10:00A.M. to 6:00P.M., Sunday 2:00P.M. to 6:00P.M.; closed Mondays, except Bank Holidays
Tube: Barbican, St Paul's, Moorgate

◆◆
MUSEUM OF THE MOVING IMAGE
South Bank Centre, Waterloo, SE1

Opened in 1988. The largest museum in the world devoted to cinema and television, tracing the history of film from the Chinese Shadow Plays of 2000BC to the latest in optical technology. Lots of hands-on exhibits: watch yourself fly over London, appear in a TV talk show, or act in a cowboy film.

Open: Tuesday to Saturday 10:00A.M. to 8:00P.M., Sunday and Bank Holidays 10:00A.M. (till 8:00P.M. June to September) to 6:00P.M.
Tube: Waterloo, Embankment

◆◆◆
NATIONAL GALLERY
Trafalgar Square, WC2
One of the world's finest collections of western European

The National Gallery was opened on its present site in 1838

paintings from about 1250 to 1900.
Quiz sheets for children
during the school vacations.
Shop (10:00A.M. to 5:40P.M. or
7:40P.M. in summer) sells books
and prints of the collection. Free.
(Note: The Sainsbury Wing, with
extra gallery space, a shop and a
restaurant, due to open in 1991.)
Open: Monday to Saturday
10:00A.M. to 6:00P.M., Sunday
2:00P.M. to 6:00P.M. Summer
evening opening until 8:00P.M. on
Wednesdays in June July and
August: talks, discussions or
musical recitals at 6:30P.M.
Tube: Charing Cross, Leicester
Square

◆◆
NATIONAL PORTRAIT GALLERY
St Martin's Place, WC2
Next to the National Gallery.
Around 9,000 portraits, arranged
chronologically, of famous
Britons from the Middle Ages to
Princess Diana. New 18th-
century galleries. Free.
Open: Monday to Friday 10:00A.M.
to 5:00P.M., Saturday 10:00A.M.
to 6:00P.M., Sunday 2:00P.M. to
6:00P.M.
Tube: Charing Cross, Leicester
Square

◆◆◆
NATURAL HISTORY MUSEUM
*Cromwell Road, South
Kensington, SW7*
Unstuffy museum with over 50
million specimens of animals
(including insects), plants and
fossils. Huge dinosaur skeletons,
'Creepy Crawly' exhibition,
videos and an exciting
interactive human biology hall (as
good as the 'Launch Pad' in the
Science Museum). The
Geological Museum is now

*The Natural History Museum –
Victorian architecture at its
exuberant best*

amalgamated with the Natural
History Museum, and the two
have a combined entrance ticket.
Open: daily 10:00A.M. to 6:00P.M.,
(Sunday 1:00P.M. to 6:00P.M.). Free
admission 4:30P.M. to 6:00P.M.
(Monday to Friday), 5:00P.M. to
6:00P.M. (weekends)
Tube: South Kensington

Laserium has a fantastic laser light/rock music show during the evenings.
Open: daily 12:20P.M. to 5:00P.M. (school vacations from 10:20A.M.). Laserium most nights telephone 071-486 2242 for programme – reservations advised.
Tube: Baker Street

◆
ROCK CIRCUS
London Pavilion, Piccadilly, W1
Opened summer 1989 by the Tussaud's company. A rock and pop audio animatronic spectacular on two floors with models of the immortals of rock and pop from Buddy Holly to Michael Jackson, plus instruments, authentic settings, spectacular lighting and sound effects. Revolving stage shows.
Open: daily 10:00A.M. to 10:00P.M.
Tube: Piccadilly Circus

◆◆
ROYAL ACADEMY OF ARTS
Burlington House, Piccadilly, W1
The home of the Fine Art Society, founded in 1768. Changing exhibitions and famous annual Summer Exhibition (see national press for details) where you can buy the work of some 1,000 artists. Shop.
Open: daily 10:00A.M. to 6:00P.M.
Tube: Piccadilly Circus, Green Park

◆◆
PLANETARIUM
Marylebone Road, NW1
Combined ticket with Madame Tussaud's. Spectacular views of the heavens with shows every 40 minutes throughout the day. The Astronomers exhibition includes wax figures of scientific luminaries such as Einstein and Galileo and three-dimensional representations of their theories and discoveries. And the

◆◆◆
SCIENCE MUSEUM
Exhibition Road, South Kensington, SW7
One of the most exciting museums for children. Original press-button Children's Gallery in the basement plus hi-tech 'Launch Pad' on the first floor providing hours of interactive

fun. Measure your heartbeat or star in your own video.
The only pity is you can't leave children on their own to get on with it! Also Space Gallery, computers, medical history, gallery of aeroplanes, films and holiday activities.
Open: Monday to Saturday

In 1871 the Cutty Sark *beat the world record by sailing from China to England in 107 days. She is now moored at Greenwich*

10:00A.M. to 6:00P.M., Sunday 11:00A.M. to 6:00P.M.
Tube: South Kensington

◆◆
TATE GALLERY
Millbank, SW1
Near Westminster Bridge, National collections of British art including 20th-century paintings and sculpture, Turners in the Clore Gallery, modern prints and changing major exhibitions. Free except for exhibitions.

Lunchtime restaurant (closed Sundays) and coffee shop.
Open: Monday to Saturday 10:00A.M. to 5:50P.M., Sunday 2:00 to 5:00P.M.
Tube: Pimlico

♦♦♦
VICTORIA AND ALBERT MUSEUM (V & A)
South Kensington, SW7
Entrances in Cromwell Road and Exhibition Road
An outstanding museum of European and Oriental decorative and fine art and design, tracing the history of glass, furniture and jewellery, textiles and dress, from early Christian times to the present day. There are exhibits from around the world, with seven miles of galleries. Also sculpture, watercolours, and Constables, plus exhibitions. Gallery talks 2:30 daily. Restaurant. Voluntary donation expected.
Open: Monday to Saturday 10:00A.M. to 5:50P.M., Sunday 2:30 to 5:50P.M.
Tube: South Kensington

Forest Hill

♦
HORNIMAN MUSEUM
London Road, Forest Hill, SE23
An Art Nouveau museum with exhibits from stuffed birds to tribal masks. Also musical instruments and aquarium.
For open air fun, there is a park with nature trail and good views of London. Changing exhibitions, lectures, workshop, concerts and courses. Café. Free.
Open: Monday to Saturday 10:30A.M. to 6:00P.M., Sunday 2:00 to 6:00P.M.
British Rail: Forest Hill (1½ miles east of Dulwich)

Greenwich

♦
CUTTY SARK AND GIPSY MOTH IV
Greenwich Pier
Two ships moored near each other on the Thames at Greenwich. In 1869 the *Cutty Sark* used to bring in tea from China and wool from Australia and was the fastest sailing clipper afloat. You can explore

WHAT TO SEE

Sigmund Freud lived here just before World War II began

above and below decks, where an exhibition explains her history. The *Gipsy Moth IV* was the boat used by Francis Chichester on the first single-handed voyage round the world in 1966/67.

Open: Cutty Sark: April to September 10:00A.M. to 6:00P.M., Sunday noon to 6:00P.M. Closes one hour earlier rest of year.

Gipsy Moth: Easter to October only; Monday to Saturday 11:00A.M. to 11:00P.M., Sunday noon to 3:00P.M. and 7:00P.M. to 10:30P.M.

British Rail: Cannon Street, Waterloo East, Charing Cross and London Bridge to Maze Hill or Greenwich or boat from Westminster, Charing Cross or Tower Piers; or foot tunnel, under the Thames from Island Gardens (Docklands Light Railway).

◆
NATIONAL MARITIME MUSEUM
Greenwich
A wonderful museum, devoted to British seafaring, partly housed in England's first Palladian-style house, designed by Inigo Jones. Navigation room with instruments, ship models, paintings, barges and galleries devoted to Lord Nelson and Captain Cook.
Open: Monday to Saturday 10:00A.M. to 6:00P.M., Sunday 2:00 to 6:00P.M.. One hour earlier in winter
British Rail: see previous entry

Hampstead

◆
FENTON HOUSE
Hampstead Grove, Hampstead, NW3
A William and Mary house built in 1693, with a collection of early musical instruments and porcelain and furniture.
Open: April to October, Saturday to Wednesday, 11:00A.M. to 6:00P.M., also March weekends 2:00P.M. to 6:00P.M.. Last admission 5:00P.M.
Tube: Hampstead

◆
FREUD MUSEUM
20 Maresfield Gardens, Hampstead, NW3
The imposing red-brick home of Sigmund Freud and his daughter Anna is now a small museum and research institute containing his furniture including the famous couch, books and collection of antiquities.
Open: Wednesday to Sunday noon to 5:00P.M.; closed Mondays and Tuesdays
Tube: Finchley Road

◆
KEATS' HOUSE
Keats Grove, Hampstead, NW3
The Regency house where Keats lived from 1818 to 1820 and where he wrote his finest poetry. Furniture of the period, his bedroom, plus cabinets of letters, manuscripts and relics relating to his friends and family, and the pretty garden in which he wrote *Ode to a Nightingale*. Keats' lover and nurse, Fanny Brawne, lived in the house next door. Voluntary donation.
Open: April to October, Monday to Friday 2:00 to 6:00P.M., Saturday 10:00A.M. to 5:00P.M., Sunday 1:00P.M. to 5:00P.M.. November to end March, Monday to Friday and Sunday 2:00P.M. to 5:00P.M., Saturday 10:00A.M. to 5:00P.M.. Closes 1:00P.M. to 2:00P.M. Saturdays
Tube: Hampstead

◆◆
KENWOOD HOUSE
The Iveagh Bequest
Hampstead Lane, Hampstead, NW3
A beautiful Robert Adam mansion overlooking the Heath, with weekend open-air lakeside jazz and symphony concerts. Lord Iveagh gave the mansion and his collection of paintings to the nation in 1927. Magnificent English 18th-century paintings, a Rembrandt self-portrait and Vermeer's *Lady Playing the Guitar*. *Free*. Restaurant, café.
Open: April to September, 10:00A.M. to 6:00P.M.; closes 2 hours earlier from October to March
Tube: Walk across the Heath from Hampstead tube; or take the 210 bus from Archway or Golders Green

Hampton Court – Richmond on
Thames

◆◆◆

HAMPTON COURT PALACE

East Molesey, Surrey

Bought by Cardinal Wolsey in
1514, this 1,000-roomed palace is
richly furnished with tapestries,
and heavily panelled with gilded
ceilings. It was enlarged by
Henry VIII, who built the Great
Hall, and again altered by Wren
in 1689. Opulent state rooms,
tapestries and famous paintings.
Set in magnificent formal
gardens, with an orangery and
famous maze.

Open: daily mid-March to mid-
October 9:30A.M. to 6:00P.M. (till
4:30P.M. rest of year). Gardens
open dawn to half an hour before
dusk

British Rail: Hampton Court (also
river trips from Westminster
Pier, Richmond and Kingston)

Twickenham

◆

MARBLE HILL HOUSE

Richmond Road, Twickenham

Palladian villa built in the 18th
century as a summer residence
for George II's mistress Henrietta
Howard, later the Countess of
Suffolk. Gilded carvings and oil
paintings. Landscaped gardens
sweeping down to the Thames
with riverside concerts on
Sunday evenings in July and
August. Free.

Open: daily; April to September
10:00A.M. to 6:00P.M. (till 4:00P.M.
rest of year)

British Rail: Waterloo to St
Margaret's; or river launches in
summer from Westminster Pier to
Richmond then by bus

*The entrance to Hampton Court
Palace, flanked by heraldic 'King's
Beasts'*

Landmarks, Cathedrals and Monuments

◆
HMS BELFAST

Morgans Lane, off Tooley Street, SE1

Huge Royal Navy cruiser from World War II. Admire it from the river (good views in front of Hays Galleria), or clamber over the seven decks to see the gun turrets and galleys.

Open: daily, mid-March to October 10:00A.M. to 6:00P.M.; rest of year till 4:30P.M.

Tube: Tower Hill, Monument or London Bridge Tower Gateway (Docklands Light Railway); or ferry from Tower Pier

◆◆
BIG BEN

Clock Tower, Palace of Westminster, SW1

Probably named after Sir Benjamin Hall, who commissioned the enormous bell and completed work on the 316ft (96m) tower in 1859. In order to climb the tower you must be in a group, be aged over 11 and have a letter of permission from your MP or embassy.

Tube: Westminster

◆◆
BUCKINGHAM PALACE

The Mall, SW1

The Queen's residence; she's at home when the Royal Standard is flying. You cannot go in unless invited to a State banquet or a garden party, but you can watch the Changing of the Guard at 11:30A.M. from early April to mid-August daily and in winter on alternate days.

Tube: Victoria, St James's Park, Green Park

Completed in 1882, the Law Courts are a superb example of Victorian Gothic architecture

◆◆◆
HOUSES OF PARLIAMENT

St Margaret Street, SW1

The Palace of Westminster includes the House of Commons and the House of Lords. You can visit the Strangers' Gallery while the House is sitting; line up outside St Stephen's entrance. Information from the Public Information Office (tel: 071 219 4272). Free.

Tube: Westminster

◆
LAW COURTS

Strand, WC2

The Royal Courts of Justice date from 1874.

Open to visitors: weekday sessions, 10:30A.M. to 1:00P.M. and 2:00 to 4:00P.M.

Tube: Temple, Aldwych

◆
LLOYD'S
Lime Street, EC3
International insurance market
housed in an eye-catching,
modern, rocket-like building
designed by Richard Rogers.
Exhibition depicting 300 years in
the City and a viewing gallery of
the Underwriting Room.
Illuminated at night. Free.
Open: Monday to Friday 10:00A.M.
to 2:30P.M.; closed weekends
Tube: Bank, Monument, Aldgate

◆
MONUMENT
Monument Street, EC3
Fluted hollow Doric column built
by Sir Christopher Wren to
commemorate the Great Fire of
London. The view from the
platform, just below the golden
urn (311 steps up), is somewhat
obscured by office blocks.
Open: April to September,
Monday to Friday 9:00A.M. to
6:00P.M., Saturday and Sunday
2:00 to 6:00P.M.. October to
March, Monday to Saturday
9:00A.M. to 4:00P.M.
Tube: Monument

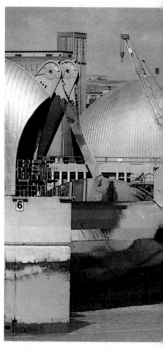

*Construction of the huge Thames
Barrier began in 1974 and was
completed in 1983*

◆
OLD BAILEY
Newgate Street, EC4
Central Criminal Court.
Open: Public Gallery Monday to
Friday 10:30A.M. to 1:00P.M. and
2:00 to 4:00P.M. when court is
sitting; closed weekends
Tube: St Paul's

◆◆◆
ST PAUL'S CATHEDRAL
Ludgate Hill, EC4
Largest and most famous church
in the City, the fourth or fifth on
the site, built by Sir Christopher
Wren. The Prince and Princess

of Wales were married there in
1981. Burial place of Nelson and
the Duke of Wellington.
Splendid views of the interior
from the Whispering Gallery.
The dome is more than 600 steps
up, but once at the top, there are
spectacular views over London.
Guided tours available but not on
Sundays and no visitors during
services. Free, but donations are
requested. A charge is made for
the crypt, galleries and
ambulatory.
Open: 8:00A.M. to 6:00P.M.
Tube: St Paul's

♦
SOUTHWARK CATHEDRAL
London Bridge, SE1
Just across London Bridge from
the City, a fine Gothic building
with the Harvard Chapel
dedicated to the founder of
Harvard University. Burial place
of Shakespeare's brother. Free.
Tube: London Bridge; or riverbus
to London Bridge

♦
10 DOWNING STREET
Off Whitehall, SW1
The official residence of the
Prime Minister; the Chancellor of
the Exchequer lives next door at
No 11. The buildings themselves
have unpretentious Georgian
facades, but have been
extensively modified inside. The
narrow, world-famous street has
a barrier at the end so you
cannot get close.
Tube: Westminster, Charing Cross

♦♦
THAMES BARRIER
Unity Way, Woolwich SE18
Between the Blackwall Tunnel
and the Woolwich Ferry. The
world's largest movable flood
barrier stretching 1700ft (520m)
across the Thames to stop water
from pouring in on London. It
consists of 10 impressive
separate movable steel gates
which when raised stand as high
as a five-storey building, as wide

WHAT TO SEE

as the opening in Tower Bridge and weigh more than a Naval destroyer. Visitors' centre, barrier cruises, riverside walk. *Open:* daily 10:30A.M. to 5:00P.M. (5:30 weekends); 8:00P.M. Wednesday to Saturday in July and August
British Rail: Charlton Station (then 15 mins walk); or river boat (1 hr 15 mins from central London or 25 mins Greenwich)

◆◆◆
TOWER BRIDGE
SE1
Opened in 1894, it took eight years to build. Splendid views from the enclosed high-level walkway across the top of the towers (elevator). Various exhibitions in the two main towers, plus Victorian engine rooms with the original steam pumps. The huge bascules are raised to let big ships through.
Open: daily; April to October 10:00A.M. to 6:30P.M., November to March 10:00A.M. to 4:45P.M.
Tube: Tower Hill, London Bridge

◆◆◆
TOWER OF LONDON
Tower Hill, EC3
William I's Tower, built on a vantage point on the river to defend the city from invaders. Its chequered past has included a prison (for the likes of Guy Fawkes and Sir Walter Raleigh), the Royal Mint and the Royal Observatory. Now the home of the Crown Jewels. The Keep is one of the earliest fortifications in western Europe. Galleries of armour and torture instruments. Yeoman Warders (popularly known as Beefeaters) wear Tudor uniform. The nightly 700-year-old Ceremony of the Keys

can be watched only by written application to the Constable's Office, Queen's House, HM Tower of London, EC3N 4AB.
Open: March to October, Monday to Saturday 9:30A.M. to 5:00P.M., Sunday 2:00P.M. to 5:00P.M.; November to February, Monday to Saturday only, 9:30A.M. to 4:00P.M.; closed Sundays in winter *Tube:* Tower Hill, or Tower Gateway (Dockland's Light Railway)

◆◆◆
WESTMINSTER ABBEY
Parliament Square, SW1
Famous kings and queens crowned and buried in the vaults, including Elizabeth I. Coronation Chair, Poet's Corner and the Stone of Scone.
Open: Nave and cloisters (free), Sunday visiting between services, weekdays 8:00A.M. to 6:00P.M. (7:45P.M. Wednesday). Royal Chapels (charge), Monday to Friday 9:00A.M. to 4:45P.M., Saturday 9:00A.M. to 2:45P.M. and 3:45 to 5:45P.M.. You can also visit the Chapter House, Pyx Chamber, Abbey Museum and College Gardens.
Tube: St James's Park, Westminster

◆◆
WESTMINSTER CATHEDRAL
Ashley Place, SW1
Behind Victoria Street. The largest and most important Roman Catholic church in England. Splendid marble and fine mosaics. (Free.) You can take an elevator to the top of the 273ft (83m) campanile (charge).
Open: bell tower, April to October 9:30A.M. to 5:00P.M., cathedral all year 7:00A.M. to 8:00P.M. *Tube:* Victoria

Tower Bridge is beautiful at any time of day

Parks, Gardens and Cemeteries

Few cities in the world can boast as many parks and open spaces, from the acres of Royal Parks, originally the hunting grounds of the Royal Palaces, to tiny grassed-over squares, a haven from the bustle of London.

Central London

◆
HOLLAND PARK

Behind Kensington High Street, a pleasant, almost suburban park, with many nannies pushing perambulators. Orangery with changing exhibitions, open-air theatre and summer concerts.
Tube: Holland Park, High Street Kensington, Kensington

WHAT TO SEE

♦♦
HYDE PARK

Once a hunting forest belonging to Henry VIII. Wide open spaces characterise Hyde Park, which is enclosed by Bayswater, Knightsbridge and Park Lane, and has the Serpentine Lake at its centre. It is the largest of the central London parks and is home to a surprisingly large range of birds. Hire a horse to ride down Rotten Row, take out a boat, swim if you can brave the British weather, or listen to the soapbox orators at Speakers' Corner.
Tube: Hyde Park Corner, Marble Arch

♦♦♦
KENSINGTON GARDENS

Merges with Hyde Park at the bridge over the Serpentine. The formal gardens of Kensington Palace, opposite the Royal Albert Hall. Don't miss the statue of Peter Pan, the Round Pond, the Orangery, feeding the ducks or the Albert Memorial.
Tube: High Street Kensington, Queensway

♦♦♦
REGENT'S PARK

The park with the most to offer: the Zoo, the open-air theatre

A detail from the Albert Memorial

(Shakespeare), a boating lake and swings for children, rowing boats for adults, cafés and Queen Mary's splendid rose garden. Alongside the park runs the Outer Circle, which is lined with elegant, columned Nash terraces.
Tube: Baker Street, Regent's Park

◆
ST JAMES'S PARK
The oldest of the Royal Parks with a lake and good views of Buckingham Palace. Alongside the Mall it joins up with Green Park, which runs along Piccadilly. Once a favourite retreat of Charles II.
Tube: Green Park, St James's Park

Outer London
◆◆
GREENWICH PARK
Overlooking the Thames with the Old Royal Observatory, original home of Greenwich Mean Time, on the crest of the ridge, and the National Maritime Museum at the bottom. This is one of the most historic of the Royal Parks, laid out by Le Nôtre for Charles II in 1662. There is a hollow oak, reputedly danced around by Elizabeth I, the deer enclosure, a boating pool and a playground.
Tube: Docklands Light Railway from Tower Gateway (Bank from summer 1991) to Island Gardens, then tunnel ('subway') under the Thames; or British Rail from Charing Cross, Waterloo East, London Bridge and Cannon Street (weekday only) to Maze Hill or Greenwich; or river boats from Westminster, Charing Cross and Tower Piers

◆
HAMPSTEAD HEATH
High open space in north London, with splendid views from Jack Straw's Castle pub and Parliament Hill, which is popular with kite flyers, Sunday afternoon walkers, dogs and joggers. Bank holiday fairground. Playground and swimming ponds. Wooded walk to Kenwood House (see separate entry) for lakeside concerts on summer weekend evenings.
Tube: Hampstead, Belsize Park

◆
HIGHGATE CEMETERY
Swains Lane, N6
Last resting place of among others, Karl Marx. Western side guided tour only, on weekends on the hour, and on summer weekdays at noon, 2:00P.M. and 4:00P.M. Photos only with permit.
Open: Eastern side April to October 10:00A.M. to 5:00P.M. rest of year till 4:00P.M.
Tube: Archway; or bus 210, C11, 143, 271

◆◆◆
KEW GARDENS (ROYAL BOTANIC GARDENS)
World-famous Royal Botanic Gardens, south of the river, with plant houses: alpines, palms, and a tropical conservatory. Splendid trees and flowering shrubs. You can have tea in the Orangery. Kew Palace is furnished in George III style.
Open: daily 9:30A.M. to between 4:00P.M. and 6:30P.M. or 8:00P.M. on Sundays depending on season
Tube: Kew Gardens; or British Rail to Kew Bridge; or buses 65, 27. Boats from Westminster Pier (summer)

WHAT TO SEE

Red deer stag – imposing resident of Richmond Park

◆
RICHMOND PARK
In southwest London, 2,500 acres used as a hunting ground by Charles I, with deer, ancient oak trees and ponds. Horses for hire, riverside walks, bicycle paths and several magnificent residences.
Tube/British Rail: Richmond

◆
SYON PARK
In Brentford, Middlesex. Around 55 acres of gardens that include a lake, rose garden, butterfly house, vintage cars, Great Conservatory and sculptures. The 16th-century house, which was remodelled by Robert Adam, is the London home of the Duke of Northumberland.
Open: Park and Gardens 9:30A.M. to 6:00P.M. or dusk
Syon House, April to September, Sunday to Thursday noon to 5:00P.M., Sunday only in October; closed November to March.
Butterfly House and the Heritage Motor Museum open daily all year 10:00A.M. to 5:30P.M.
Tube: Gunnersbury; then take the bus 237 or 267 to Brent Lea Gate

PEACE AND QUIET

Wildlife and Countryside in and around London
by Paul Sterry

At first glance, the centre of London, like many other capitals, may not seem the most suitable place to observe wildlife: house sparrows, starlings and pigeons are often the only creatures to be seen. However, visit the right locations or travel as little as 30 miles (48km) from the city centre and a fascinating array of plants and animals lies waiting to be discovered.

Even the central Royal Parks, such as St James's Park and Hyde Park, have squirrels and woodpigeons, and the presence of tame birds on their lakes lures wild birds into these rather unnatural settings. The same is true of London Zoo, set in Regent's Park; sometimes it is difficult to tell the captive creatures from the wild ones. Examples of most habitats typical of southern England lie within a day's journey of the capital. The remains of once great hunting forests can be found at Windsor and Epping and freshwater habitats, from lakes to rivers, abound, many being associated with the course of the Thames, which bisects the city. Even specialised and wildlife-rich habitats such as heathland and chalk grassland lie close to the city and are well worth a visit.

The Royal Parks of Central London

In the heart of the capital, the Royal Parks provide a haven of comparative solitude away from the hustle and bustle of city life. The vegetation of these parks is almost entirely dictated by man and the wildlife often exotic and introduced, but the presence of animals which are tolerant of humans often draws in more interesting wild species.

St James's Park is home to ubiquitous house sparrows which are bold enough to feed from people's hands, and flocks of feral pigeons come and go from nearby Trafalgar Square. A surprising resident of both this park and nearby Hyde Park is the woodpigeon. It is not persecuted here as it is in the rest of Britain and consequently has become extremely confiding.

Both St James's Park and Hyde Park contain lakes and ponds and, of these, the Serpentine is the most interesting. The lake winds its way along the northern side of Hyde Park and it contains numerous fish which are food for fish-eating birds.

To explore the Serpentine, park on the northern shore just off The Ring, near Serpentine Bridge. Walk around the edge of the water and around the Long Water as well. Look for moorhens and coots among the tufted ducks, mallards and Canada geese. Grey herons are sometimes seen early in the morning and great crested grebes nest on the island near the Boat House. In spring, pairs of grebes perform elaborate displays on the water prior to mating and nest building. The parking lot is also a good spot from which to explore the open parkland and scrub. Small patches of woodland in Hyde Park and adjoining Kensington Gardens sometimes

PEACE AND QUIET

harbour migrant birds such as spotted flycatchers, redstarts and willow warblers in spring, while jays are resident throughout the year. They will often come and investigate those visitors who seem a likely source of food, often with bold grey squirrels in hot pursuit. These charming animals were introduced from North America, but have adapted extremely well to British woodlands and urban environments. Grey squirrels are fascinating creatures to watch as they dextrously use their paws to eat, but be careful not to get too close because they can, and do, bite if provoked.

Richmond Park

Lying just south of the Thames in west London, Richmond Park is the most 'natural' of the Royal Parks and without doubt the one which holds the most wildlife interest. Famous for its deer, which are numerous and obligingly tame, the park is an enclave of attractive, rolling countryside set among the sprawling suburbs, and is popular with Londoners and visitors alike.

Richmond Park has ponds, open grassland with scattered trees and areas of more mature woodland. Rhododendron thickets provide a wonderful flowering display in June which attracts the admiration of both visitors and pollinating insects. Insects are not confined to the flowers, however, and a careful search of the foliage may reveal the amazingly colourful rhododendron leafhopper, as well as oak bush crickets and

speckled bush crickets.

Despite the houses and tower blocks which surround and almost overlook the park, the birdlife is surprisingly rich. Kestrels are frequently seen hovering over the grassland on the look-out for scurrying voles, and spotted flycatchers, great spotted woodpeckers, tits, nuthatches and treecreepers can be found in the wooded areas. The ponds sometimes attract interesting wildfowl and reed warblers have been known to attempt to nest around their margins.

As soon as you enter the park, you cannot fail to notice the deer. Sizeable herds of both red and fallow deer roam the grassland, and because they are forever confined within its boundaries, they are easily seen throughout the year. In the autumn, the red deer in particular are at their most spectacular: dominant stags with huge sets of antlers gather together their harems of hinds, and bellow warnings at other males. Visit the park on a cold October morning and you will be treated to the memorable sound of stags 'belling', their breath steaming in the damp air, and the sight of crashing antlers as rivals do battle.

For good views of the deer, park in designated spots at Robin Hood Gate and walk towards Pen Ponds. They are usually close to the road and are easiest to see on the north side where the grassland is more open. However, the lusher vegetation to the south provides a more appropriate setting. If you find a young deer in spring, leave it alone: otherwise the mother may desert.

One of the ancient oaks in Windsor Great Park

Windsor Great Park and Virginia Water

Despite its popularity, Windsor Great Park, which lies to the west of London, is still a fine example of mature English parkland. The landscape is dotted with stately trees and, nestling within its woodlands, the tranquil surface of Virginia Water reflects its leafy surroundings like a mirror. Throughout the park, ancient oaks with gnarled and twisted trunks and withered looking branches play host to large numbers of insects, including several rare species of beetles not known elsewhere in the country. During July and August, purple hairstreak butterflies flit among the foliage, while at ground level, speckled woods and small tortoiseshells are common.

PEACE AND QUIET

If you are lucky, you might see a purple hairstreak butterfly in Windsor Great Park

The birds also benefit from the variety and age of the trees. Diminutive lesser spotted woodpeckers feed unobtrusively throughout the park, while green and great spotted woodpeckers are conspicuous and noisy, making them easier to locate. Kestrels hunt over the open ground and, during the summer months, hobbies are occasionally seen as they scythe through the air in search of swallows and house martins.

The woodlands around Virginia Water are renowned for being one of the most reliable places in the counties around London to see hawfinches. Normally rather shy and elusive birds, hawfinches are frequently found in the vicinity of hornbeam trees close to the parking lot, and their massive, seed-cracking bills give them an unmistakable silhouette when perched high in a tree.

For a lovely circular walk, park either in the large parking lot beside the A30 or in the parking lot beside the A329 at Blacknest. From the shores of the lake Canada geese and ducks can be seen; this is the best place in England to see mandarin ducks. Carp, tench and other fish can be seen spawning from the bridges in the early summer. In October, when the leaves and seeds of most trees fall to the ground, and thereafter for the rest of the winter, chaffinches, bramblings and the occasional hawfinch can be seen feeding on the woodland floor.

During the winter months, this variety of birds is sometimes joined by small numbers of winter visitors such as scaup, goldeneye and smew. These are particularly easy to see as the water begins to freeze because the birds become concentrated as the area of open water reduces.

The Surrey Heaths

Lying to the southwest of London, the landscape of Surrey varies from mature woodland to chalk grassland. Above all, however, it is the open heathland for which the county is best known and, despite being so close to the capital, there are still areas, such as Chobham Common, which have escaped housing development. The heathers (from which the habitat gets its name) and the gorse are the glory of the heathlands and, from June to August, turn the landscape into seas of yellows and purples.

Although heathlands may look natural, their appearance is actually due to generations of tree clearance by man. The resulting nutrient-poor, acidic soils have an extremely specialised flora, with ling, bell heather, cross-leaved heath and gorse predominating, interspersed with tussocks of the characteristic purple moor-grass. In wetter areas, beautiful yellow spikes of bog asphodel grow among the carpet of *Sphagnum* moss, and carnivorous sundew plants supplement their diet by digesting insects caught on their sticky leaves.

Heathlands are renowned for their spiders, misty autumn mornings highlighting the tell-tale webs and strands of silk with dew. Insects also abound and colourful emperor moths are on the wing in March and April, while July and August are the months for grayling and silver-studded blue butterflies and numerous species of dragonfly and damselfly. Among the low vegetation, mottled grasshoppers hop to safety and bog bush crickets clamber among the cross-leaved heath. The insect life supports a variety of birds, with stonechats and pipits being particularly conspicuous. Among the larger clumps of gorse, the more secretive Dartford warbler, long since extinct in its place of discovery in Kent, scolds intruders into its territory.

Emperor moths are big and spectacular and not uncommon on heathlands in spring

Although they prefer to skulk in the cover of vegetation, during March and April, males often perch aloft on the tops of gorse spikes, singing for all they are worth.

To visit Chobham Common, park in one of the parking lots off the Chobham Road (B383) near Chertsey. Thursley Common is another fine example of southern heathland. Park on the west side of the common, which lies between Farnham and Haslemere, off the A287. Headley Heath has a parking lot to the west of the B2033 near Leatherhead.

Reservoirs

Vast quantities of water are consumed by Londoners. To quench this thirst, numerous reservoirs have been built around the outskirts of the city, these benefiting not only the human population but also large

If the water is very low, green sandpipers might stop off to feed in muddy reservoir bottoms

numbers of birds. These in turn lure birdwatchers, who find the variety of species and numbers of birds they offer as good as, if not better than, many rural areas. Most notable and easily accessible of the reservoirs is Staines, situated under the flight path of many of the jets which leave Heathrow. Although the noise may detract from some people's enjoyment, it certainly seems to do little to upset the birds, who carry on feeding regardless. From the central causeway which separates the two halves of the reservoir, huge numbers of ducks can be seen during the winter months, with unusual birds such as red-necked grebe and black-throated diver being recorded in most years.

Black-throated divers are large water birds which swim low in the water. Although more usually associated with coastal waters, they regularly turn up inland on areas of water with lots of fish. Black-throated divers are superficially similar to cormorants but lack the hooked-tip bill of this species.

From March to May, Staines Reservoir is a good spot to watch for passage migrants such as sand martins, swallows, swifts and black terns. Rarities such as white-winged black terns and whiskered terns appear occasionally and the list of unusual birds is not confined to water-loving species.

Every now and then, the water authorities have to drain one or other of the reservoirs in order to remove the build-up of silt. This rich expanse of mud, teeming with small invertebrates, soon attracts waders such as dunlins and redshanks.

To visit Staines Reservoir, park in one of the residential roads off Town Lane – this heads north from the A30 to the west of the reservoir – and walk to the causeway. Brent Reservoir is another good spot to visit. It lies near the junction of the North Circular Road and Edgeware Road in West Hendon. Park off Church Lane.

The North Downs and Box Hill

Within easy reach of London, the North Downs, a long ridge of chalk running east to west through Surrey, provides fabulous views over rolling English countryside. The North Downs Way provides long-distance walks, but for those with less time to spare, the wildlife and scenery of Box Hill Country Park near Dorking is particularly rewarding. Although the park suffers greatly from public pressure, the range of plants and animals within its boundaries is immense.

Centuries of woodland clearance and sheep grazing have combined to produce the close-cropped grassland so typical of chalky soils. On this land, known as 'downland', constant nibbling by sheep and rabbits has encouraged a rich diversity of flowering plants which would otherwise be crowded out by the grasses. During the summer months, yellow rattle, marjoram, thyme, sainfoin, kidney vetch and knapweeds provide a kaleidoscope of colour, and attract insects such as hover-flies, burnet moths, and

Yellow rattle – a showy plant of downland in early summer. The ripe seed pods rattle when shaken

butterflies including silver-spotted skipper, common blue and chalkhill blue.

In southern England, orchids are the real botanical speciality of chalk downland, with many colourful and extraordinary species being found around Box Hill. Purple spikes of fragrant orchids and the aptly named pyramidal orchid grow alongside the diminutive greenish-yellow plants of musk orchids, while where the scrub provides a degree of shade, common twayblades and man orchids can sometimes be found.

PEACE AND QUIET

Many of the downland invertebrates are also unique to the chalky soils, and snails are often abundant, the calcium providing building materials for their shells. Humbug-like shells of white-lipped and brown-lipped snails are conspicuous, while immense edible snails, introduced to Britain by the Romans, are best seen on damp or overcast days among the scrub.

On many slopes on the North Downs, scrub and woodland still persist. Box Hill gains its name from the box trees which predominate in some areas, but elder and yew are also common. To find Box Hill Country Park parking lot, follow signs from the A24 just to the north of Dorking or from the A25 between Dorking and Reigate. Other superb areas of downland can be found at Ranmore Common. The parking lot is located on the minor road which runs from Dorking to East Horsley. The area is particularly well known for the wide range of butterflies that can be found during spring and summer.

The Thames Estuary

On its journey from London to the North Sea, the Thames fans out to form an extensive estuary bordered on the north by Essex and on the south by Kent. Although at times bleak and forbidding, and often industrialised, this habitat is the winter home to thousands of birds and a nursery ground for many commercially important species of fish. Access to the marshes is often difficult, but at Two-Tree Island near Southend in Essex and from Cliffe to High Halstow in Kent good views of the mudflats and their teeming birdlife can be had.

Much of coastal Kent and Essex is protected from floods and gales by sea walls, and to the naturalist both the landward and the seaward sides are of interest. Inland, the coastal marshes are grazed by cattle and are breeding grounds for redshank, snipe and yellow wagtail in the summer, while in the winter, short-eared owls and hen harriers hunt for small mammals. Hen harriers are graceful birds of prey that feed by quartering the ground. Both sexes have a conspicuous white rump. The plumage of the male is grey while that of the female is brown. Hen harriers breed in upland areas of England and Scotland.

The vast areas of mud and silt which the Thames has deposited over the centuries become exposed at low tide and provide a rich feeding ground for birds. Shelduck dabble in the shallow water for small molluscs, while brent geese, visitors from Arctic Russia, alternate between feeding grounds in the creeks and the close-cropped fields behind the sea walls. Huge numbers of dunlin, knot, grey plover, redshank, curlew and godwit probe the mud for lugworms and molluscs, taking to the wind in tight flocks at the slightest disturbance.

Northward Hill is an RSPB reserve which protects part of the north Kent marshes as well as oak woodland. It lies northeast of Rochester and can be reached on Northwood Road from High Halstow village. Grey herons and nightingales breed here and long-

*Marshes such as this one in Kent
are excellent for birds*

eared owls are seen in winter.
On the Isle of Sheppey is Elmley,
another RSPB reserve. A
signposted track heads east from
the A249 1 mile north of Kingsferry
Bridge. There are grazing marshes
and freshwater scrapes here
which attract large numbers of
waders and wildfowl, especially
during the winter months.

Epping Forest

Only a short distance from the
centre of London, Epping Forest
is an extensive area of ancient
woodland with wide forest rides,
established many centuries ago
as a royal hunting forest. Sadly, it
no longer harbours the deer
which once provided sport for
kings, the disturbance caused
by increased public pressure
having driven them away. The
decline in tree management has
also had an adverse effect on the
diversity of the forest's wildlife,
especially its birds and
mammals. Despite this, however,
Epping Forest still has
magnificent trees and is a
wonderful escape from the city
for both the casual stroller and
those more interested in
observing the plant and animal
life of the woodland.

PEACE AND QUIET

Epping Forest. It is difficult to believe that this great tract of ancient woodland is right on London's doorstep

During the winter months, flocks of redpolls, occasionally joined by small numbers of siskins, feed among the high branches of the trees. The flocks often form loose associations with blue tits, coal tits, long-tailed tits and goldcrests, whose high-pitched calls attract the attention of the observer. Since the trees lack leaves at this time of year, following the movements of the birds is comparatively easy.

Winter is also the best season to observe the hawfinches of Epping Forest which, as elsewhere in Britain, are generally associated with hornbeam trees. Among European passerines, their massive bill is the only one powerful enough to crack the tree's hard seeds and the loud cracking sound can sometimes even help locate the birds. The buds burst into leaf in April and May just as many migrant birds are arriving from Africa. Whitethroats, blackcaps and willow warblers are common

information about the Forest and its long history of association with man. The area with the most wildlife interest is in Great Monk Wood, which harbours ancient trees. Woodland birds, butterflies and fungi are numerous.

The Thames
Although its role in the life of the city has dwindled over the centuries, the Thames is still a focal point and has much to offer the visitor. Beyond Docklands, the river opens out to form the vast Thames Estuary which is the haunt of thousands of wintering birds, while up-river towards Henley it gradually becomes more attractive as waterside vegetation and lush agricultural land appear along its banks. Once so polluted that no life survived in the waters that flowed through London, the Thames is now undergoing a slow process of being cleaned up and fish are beginning to recolonise. A variety of birds can also be seen along its course in central London, the most conspicuous being black-headed gulls, which are present for most of the year except the height of summer. Flocks of these noisy birds often include herring gulls or even common gulls, all of which commute between the Thames and London's many reservoirs and parkland lakes.

As the banks of the Thames become more rural, kingfishers occasionally fly by in a dazzling flash of blue and red and it is possible to see graceful mute swans more and more frequently.

songsters, and colourful redstarts flit amongst the dappled branches. As hole-nesting birds, redstarts benefit from the holes left in the tree trunks by fallen branches and ancient pollards but they often have to compete for nest sites with nuthatches and woodpeckers, who have similar preferences.

Epping Forest lies northwest of Loughton. There are several parking lots off the A11(T) as well as on minor roads through the forest. The Conservation Centre at High Beach provides

These stately birds are considered Crown property and have benefited from the protection this has provided. In the spring, large nests of twigs and grasses are built among the riverside vegetation and are fiercely guarded by the male bird, which is known as a cob. Along the course of the Thames from Wraysbury near Heathrow to Reading, there is a mosaic of hundreds of gravel pits. To explore the network of gravel pits around Wraysbury, explore the minor road around Horton, Wraysbury, Datchet and Hythe End to the west of the M25. There are extensive gravel pit workings around Theale, which lies to the east of Reading. Explore the minor roads around Burghfield, Theale and Sheffield Bottom. Many of the best lakes can be viewed from the road.

Where these gravel pits have not yet filled with water, they provide the ideal conditions for one of Britain's scarcest breeding waders. Little-ringed plovers lay their camouflaged eggs on the pebbly ground where they are almost impossible to spot. Adult birds, with their yellow eye-rings, are also inconspicuous as they quietly incubate the eggs until the young hatch.

Freshwater Habitats

Less than 25 miles (40 km) north of central London, the valleys of the rivers Chess and Lea offer a rich variety of natural freshwater habitats which contrast markedly with the formal appearance of the ponds and lakes in the city's parks. With both flowing rivers and still waters of marshes and lakes, the birdlife is fascinating throughout the year and from May to August colourful flowers catch the eye. The River Chess is an attractive, shallow river which between Rickmansworth and Chorley is bordered with rich waterside vegetation. Metallic-blue damselflies and mayflies dance around the bushes and family parties of mute swans regally paddle up and down, in places such as Chenies becoming quite tame and inquisitive.

Patches of thick vegetation sometimes harbour breeding sedge warblers and overhanging branches serve as convenient perches for colourful kingfishers. During the winter months, small numbers of green sandpipers, easily recognised in flight by their white rumps, feed along the river margins. They also frequent the margins of gravel pits and man-made lakes such as Stocker's Lake near Rickmansworth.

Further east, the Lea Valley also holds interesting freshwater habitats. The RSPB's reserve at Rye House Marsh near Hoddesdon has a public birdwatching hide overlooking an interesting area of marsh. Both reed and sedge warblers sing from the cover of the reeds during May and June while common terns, which breed on man-made rafts in the reserve's pools, scream overhead. During migration time, swallows, martins and black terns pass through the area and a wide selection of waders such as green and common sandpipers, redshank, ruff and little-ringed plovers put in brief appearances. During the winter months, the reserve is frequented by good numbers of wildfowl, gulls and waders, such as snipe and jack snipe.

Rye House Marsh lies to the east of Hoddesdon in Hertfordshire and there is a parking lot opposite Rye House railway station. The Old River Lea is another good wetland area and is especially rich in dragonflies. It can be reached by crossing footbridges from Waltham Abbey in Hertfordshire. There are numerous gravel pits to the north of nearby Cheshunt.

Water rail – retiring inhabitant of marshes and watersides

Kew Gardens

An entrance fee allows access to the world-famous Royal Botanic Gardens at Kew, which have been open to the public since 1841. To anyone interested in botany, the gardens are a paradise, containing plants from all over the world, and with over 30,000 species and varieties of plant on display, Kew provides an endless source of interest. Flowers are grown both outdoors and indoors, within elaborate showpiece greenhouses, so there is plenty to see all year round. Spring, however, is especially colourful with blooms of every conceivable hue on show.

PEACE AND QUIET

In contrast to the wonderful displays of flowers in the formal borders and those in the botanical study areas, part of the garden has been devoted to a more natural setting and was originally laid out by Capability Brown. Here the visitor can stroll through attractive, lakeside woodland, the ground carpeted with flowers early in the year, and be serenaded by woodland birds. Because they are not persecuted, many species have become remarkably confiding, and jays and woodpigeons in particular seem to have little fear of people.

Kew Gardens. As well as the various glasshouses, there are 300 acres of grounds to explore here

FOOD AND DRINK

Restaurants

Restaurants with the best food in the capital are generally pricey, especially in the evening. But there are exceptions and at lunchtime many offer the chance to try a fixed-price menu at a fraction of the evening price. A selection of outstanding restaurants is given here.

Alastair Little, 49 Frith Street, W1 (tel: 071 734 5183). A small, stylish, street-level, café-like restaurant, with bare black tables and a daily changing menu that roams Europe and further afield. Reasonably expensive (cash only). Closed Saturday lunchtimes and Sundays.

L'Arlequin, 123 Queenstown Road, Battersea, SW8 (tel: 071 622 0555). Small, south London restaurant (just over Chelsea Bridge) with dreary décor. Christian Delteil has little time for matching crockery or fussy garnishes but produces largely well-executed French dishes and desserts deserving of an Egon Ronay Restaurant of the Year award. Cheap set-lunch menu, otherwise very expensive. Popular with intellectuals. Closed weekends.

Bibendum, Michelin House (First Floor), 81 Fulham Road, SW3 (tel: 071 581 5817). Art Deco style first-floor, elegant, fashionable restaurant full of animated celebrities, with chef Simon Hopkinson rejecting *nouvelle cuisine* in favour of regional, usually classic French dishes, though fish and chips or rice pudding may be on the changing menu at lunchtime. Open daily.

Chez Nico, 35 Great Portland

M. Bibendum oversees his restaurant

Street, W1 (tel: 071 436 8846). Chef-proprietor Nico Ladenis recently exchanged his Victoria backwater (see Very Simply Nico) for this unlikely location near Oxford Circus (and the 'Simply' for 'Chez'). To eat there is an experience. Simply one of the best restaurants in London, and Nico won't mind at all if you applaud. Expensive. Closed weekends.

The Four Seasons, Inn on the Park Hotel, Park Lane, W1 (tel: 071 499 0888). A dimly lit, florid, palm-filled, fussy room that somewhat detracts from the inventiveness of Bruno Loubet's classic cooking. Rather expensive, but Loubet is touted as the chef of the 1990s.

FOOD AND DRINK

Le Gavroche, 43 Upper Brook Street, W1 (tel: 071 408 0881). Owned by the famous Roux brothers. Serious French restaurant with an impressive menu taking in both simple dishes and elaborate creations. Very special and very expensive. Closed weekends.

Harvey's, 2 Bellvue Road, Wandsworth, SW17 (tel: 081 672 0114). Owned by the inspired young Marco Pierre White who has invested his future in a charming, pretty restaurant overlooking Wandsworth Common. He is already hailed as one of the best chefs in Britain, and his dishes are a colourful canvas of the finest ingredients, with a clarity of vision and taste few of his contemporaries can emulate. Reasonable lunch menu, and less expensive than most. Closed Sundays, lunch not served Saturdays.

Le Mazarin, 30 Winchester Street, SW1 (tel: 071 828 3366). Intimate, small restaurant, in a warren-like basement, owned by chef René Bajard, a Roux brother's protégé, who offers three set menus, including a *menu gastronome*. Closed Sundays and Mondays.

The Oak Room, in Le Meridien Hotel, 21 Piccadilly, W1 (tel: 071 734 8000). A rather grand, gilt and mirrored, baroque banqueting hall with an international feel and a rather loud pianist, offering *cuisine creative, traditionelle* or *gourmand* and changing specialities. Very expensive.

Le Soufflé, on the ground floor of the Inter-Continental Hotel, 1 Hamilton Place, W1 (tel: 071 409 3131). Arguably the best hotel food in London. A small,

Exterior style reflects the interior qualities of La Tante Claire

tastefully decorated dining room, where chef Peter Kromberg specialises in imaginative soufflés as well as outstanding French dishes.

Sutherlands, 45 Lexington Street, W1 (tel: 071 434 3401). A new wave Soho restaurant, stylish down to its black menus and waiters in city-striped shirts. A long narrow room. Set menus, superb breads, soups served at the table in copper pans. Immaculate presentation. Reasonably expensive.

La Tante Claire, 68-69 Royal Hospital Road, SW3 (tel: 071 352 6045). Pierre Koffmann is at the helm of this small temple of gastronomy offering consistently high standards and good-value lunches, otherwise very expensive. Closed weekends.

The following is a mixed bag of restaurants (also see separate sections for **Vegetarian** and **Ethnic**) selected for their better than average food, ambience and good value.

Expensive:
In Hotels. The legendary, oak-panelled restaurant in the **Connaught** in Carlos Place (tel: 071 499 7070) and the **Savoy's** Grill Room (tel: 071 836 4343), much loved by businessmen, are both very expensive. The long-awaited lavishly restored and refurbished **Dorchester** in Park Lane (tel: 071 629 8888) has a New Oriental restaurant to complement the Grill and Terrace. The Chelsea Room in the **Hyatt Carlton Tower,** Cadogan Place (tel: 071 235 5411) near Harrods, is a good choice for lunch (including wine); or try the club-like, wood-panelled Rib Room which specialises in roast meat and shellfish. **Dukes Hotel** (tel: 071 491 4840), tucked away in

FOOD AND DRINK

St James's Place, offers traditional English and French food (from 6:00P.M. onwards), immaculately presented in a small formal dining room. The Causerie at **Claridge's** in Brook Street, W1 (tel: 071 629 8860) is much loved by Royalty who come for the comfortable, elegant setting and the smörgåsbord lunch. The restaurant also offers early evening (available from 5:30P.M.) buffets.

With Dancing. The **Savoy's** opulent River Restaurant (tel: 071 836 4343) overlooks the Thames and has a band most nights. There is also dancing (on Saturdays) in the sumptuous Louis XVI style French baroque dining room at the **Ritz** (tel: 071 493 8181) and big-band dancing in the Ritz's Palm Court (where they serve afternoon teas) on Friday and Saturday nights.

Tea at the Ritz

Reasonable:

Caprice, Arlington House, Arlington Street, SW1 (tel: 071 629 2239). Chic, black and white brasserie with a large menu, in the heart of Mayfair, which attracts celebrities, especially for Sunday brunch. Open every day until midnight.

Chez Moi, 1 Addison Avenue, Holland Park, W11 (tel: 071 603 8267). Old-fashioned, unchanging French restaurant that's been in the food guides for over 20 years.

Clarke's, 124 Kensington Church Street, W8 (tel: 071 221 9225). Sally Clarke, the chef-owner, offers a no-choice, nightly changing menu and a short choice at lunch in her modern two-floor restaurant. She char grills in the open-plan kitchen and offers Californian, Italian or Japanese dishes and English farmhouse cheeses (sold next door). Closed weekends.

Kensington Place, 201 Kensington Church Street, W8 (tel: 071 727 3184). Noisy, hi-tech, street-level, fashionable brasserie with an eclectic menu. Open from noon to 11:45P.M.

The Kingfisher Restaurant, Halcyon Hotel, 81 Holland Park Avenue, W11 (tel: 071 221 5411). In a comfortable garden room with a York stone floor and an open courtyard for sunny days. Good value light lunches.

Langan's Brasserie, Stratton Street, W1 (tel: 071 493 6437). Michael Caine's winning brasserie off Piccadilly, on two floors. Large, noisy and fashionable, with photographers outside ready to snap the inevitable celebrities. Closed Saturday lunchtimes, Sundays.

The Terrace Garden, Le Meridien Hotel, Piccadilly, W1 (tel: 071 734 8000). Exotic fern and tree-filled split-level conservatory overlooking Piccadilly, relatively inexpensive snacks and meals served all day from 7:00A.M. to 11:30P.M. Pianist entertains most nights.

Very Simply Nico, 48a Rochester Row, SW1 (tel: 071 630 8061). A cheaper, simpler version of Chez Nico, with Nico's sous chef in command. Closed Sundays.

For Fish. The Pierre Martin chain of fish restaurants has been well established for over 15 years. Cannes-type atmosphere and dishes that include a vast cork platter of seafood, nestling on a crinkly bed of seaweed. Not overly expensive, the staff and everything down to the butter are all French. His restaurants include: **La Bouillabaisse**, 116 Finborough Road, SW10 (tel: 071 370 4199); **La Croisette**, 168 Ifield Road, SW10 (tel: 071 373 3694); **Le Suquet** (the most popular with celebrities, ask for a table downstairs), 104 Draycott Avenue, SW3 (tel: 071 581 1785) and **Le Quai St Pierre**, 7 Stratford Road, W8 (tel: 071 937 6388).

For Oysters. There are oyster bars at **Wiltons**, 55 Jermyn Street, SW1 (tel: 071 629 9955) or at **Green's**, 36 Duke Street, SW1 (tel: 071 930 4566), which also has a champagne bar.

Inexpensive:

There are relatively few good, cheap restaurants in London, but you can often eat cheaply in Indian, Italian and Chinese restaurants (see separate **Ethnic** section).

FOOD AND DRINK

Otherwise try:

Chelsea Kitchen, 98 King's Road, SW3 (tel: 071 589 1330). Hearty basic cooking that has been giving sustenance to shoppers and students for over 30 years. No reservations, shared tables. Open 8:00A.M. to 11:45P.M. (Sunday from noon).

The Chinoiserie, Hyatt Carlton, Cadogan Place, SW1 (tel: 071 235 5411). Ground-floor, comfortable, though formal lounge, where snacks and light meals are served from 8:00A.M. to midnight. A harpist plays at teatime, a pianist during lunch and dinner.

Chinon, 25 Richmond Way, W14 (tel: 071 602 5968). Tiny French restaurant in a parade of shops in Shepherd's Bush. Excellent value if you stick to the no-choice set menu. Closed Saturday lunchtimes and Sundays.

Fields, 5 St Martin's Place, WC2 (tel: 071 839 4342). Enormous brick-vaulted coffee bar/ restaurant in the crypt, serving hot dishes, coffee and cakes and with a cheap set menu. Profits go towards the church. Good for pre-theatre suppers. Open 10:00A.M. to 8:30P.M. (7:30P.M. Sunday).

Pollo, 20 Old Compton Street, W1 (tel: 071 734 5917). Cheap and cheerful long-standing Soho Italian restaurant.

Stockpot, 40 Panton Street, SW1 (tel: 071 839 5142). Hearty meals at rock-bottom prices; very studenty. The Stockpot at 6 Basil Street (tel: 071 589 8627) in Knightsbridge SW3 is similar.

Surinder's, 109 Westbourne Park Road, W2 (tel: 071 229 8968). Outstanding value. Small formal restaurant with pretty peach décor and short daily changing set menu that may include lobster or *foie gras*. Closed Sundays and Mondays. Dinner only (also lunch on Fridays).

Vegetarian

Cranks, 8 Marshall Street, W1 (tel: 071 437 5117). Popular café, one of several branches. Open 8:00A.M. to 10:30P.M.

Inigo Jones, 14 Garrick Street, WC2 (tel: 071 836 6456). Very expensive French restaurant with outstanding *menu potager*.

Leith's, 92 Kensington Park Road, W11 (tel: 071 229 4481). Modern expensive restaurant with excellent selection of vegetarian dishes using ingredients (often organic) from Prue Leith's own Cotswold farm. Dinner only.

Neal's Yard Bakery, 6 Neal's Yard, WC2 (tel: 071 836 5199). Covent Garden hang-out for serious vegetarians (in among the health food shops). Cheap. Open 10:30A.M. to 8:00P.M. Monday to Friday (5:00P.M. Wednesday) and till 4:30P.M. on Saturdays.

Ethnic

Ethnic restaurants are generally cheap, provided their owners haven't inflated their prices just because they've replaced paper tablecloths with linen, lager with wine, and added potted plants and piped music to the décor. You stand a good chance of getting a table without reservations and of finding somewhere open early or late. Of the thousands of restaurants, a selection is listed below by nationality (with phone numbers where reservations are necessary).

American. The **Hard Rock Café**, 150 Old Park Lane, W1 (near Hyde Park Corner). Long lines. Very noisy and cheap. No reservations. Open noon to

FOOD AND DRINK

Eat American at the Hard Rock Café

12:30A.M. (1:00A.M. Friday and Saturday) every day. **Joe Allen's** basement in Covent Garden's Exeter Street down an alley near the Aldwych (tel: 071 836 0651) is popular with actors after the show and is open until 12:45A.M. **Henry J Bean's**, 195 King's Road, in Chelsea SW3 (tel: 071 352 9255) is done out like a 1950s American bar; they serve whisky, cocktails, beer, burgers and other dishes. The sophisticated **Fifty One Fifty One**, Chelsea Cloisters, Sloane Avenue, SW3 (tel: 071 730 5151) serves New Orleans, Cajun and Creole dishes to the rich and famous. Reasonably priced lunchtimes menus, early suppers from 6:30P.M.; otherwise expensive.

Chinese. London's Chinatown centres around Soho's pedestrianised Gerrard Street with its Oriental gateways, shops selling Chinese goods and books, and Chinese doctors. Many restaurants stay open late and although you may have to wait in line to get in you don't usually have to reserve a table. **Poons** at 4 Leicester Street, WC2 (tel: 071 437 1528) specialises in wind-dried food. **Chuen Cheng Ku** is vast, has been at 17 Wardour Street (tel: 071 437 3433) for over 20 years, and its reputation as the best *dim sum* palace is rivalled only by the even larger 600-seater **New World** in Gerrard Place (tel: 071 734 0677). **Fung Shing** at 15 Lisle Street (tel: 071 437 1539) is smarter than most while the largely

FOOD AND DRINK

Szechuan (spicy) **Dragon's Nest** at 58 Shaftesbury Avenue (tel: 071 437 3119) is somewhat more ambitious than its neighbours. If you're in a hurry, **Wong Kei**, on three floors, at 41 Wardour Street (tel: 071 437 8408) is quick, with brisk, no-nonsense service and a busy atmosphere. If you fancy *dim sum* for breakfast, the hi-tech **China Joe**, 93 Old Brompton Road (tel: 071 581 9219) opens at 7:30A.M. Monday to Saturday and from noon on Sunday. Insomniacs might like to know that **Yung's**, 23 Wardour Street (tel: 071 439 7511) and **China China**, a new fast-food restaurant at 3 Gerrard Street (tel: 071 437 3864) are both open until about 4:00A.M.

Outside Chinatown, the best Chinese restaurants are usually more formal and more expensive. One of the first was **Ken Lo's Memories of China** at 67–69 Ebury Street, SW1 (tel: 071 730 7734). **Ken Lo's Memories of China**, Harbour Yard, Chelsea Harbour, SW10 (tel: 071 352 4953), has views of boats, a menu that roams the regions and a reasonably priced *dim sum* brasserie open throughout the day. Ken Lo himself sometimes cooks Sunday brunch. There are three branches of the 'monosodium-free' fashionable **Zen** restaurants, all with modern European designer décor: **Zen Chelsea** in Chelsea Cloisters, Sloane Avenue, SW3 (tel: 071 589 1781) was the first, followed by **Zenw 3** (with its cascading waterfall) at 83 Hampstead High Street, NW3 (tel: 071 794 7863) and **Zen Central** in Mayfair at 20–22 Queen Street, W1 (tel: 071 629 8103).

Almost like an outpost of an old Empire: the Bombay Brasserie

Greek/Cypriot. Few restaurants excel. In Swiss Cottage, **Zita**, 31 College Crescent, NW3 (tel: 071 483 2924) is a remarkably friendly, family-owned restaurant, with an exciting, French-influenced menu and fish specialities (closed Saturday lunchtimes and Sundays). In several restaurants in Charlotte Street, W1, you can throw plates

Indian. Among the best are the **Red Fort** in Soho's Dean Street (tel: 071 437 2525) and its new, popular with the media, sister **Jamdani** at 34 Charlotte Street, W1 (tel: 071 636 1178), where they specialise in unusual dishes. Equally sophisticated in a decadent colonial sort of way is the palm-strewn **Bombay Brasserie**, opposite Gloucester Road tube station, in Courtfield Close, Courtfield Road, SW7 (tel: 071 370 4040), with its evening and Sunday lunchtime piano music. Or try **Lal Qila**, 117 Tottenham Court Road, W1 (tel: 071 387 4570), where they specialise in North Indian dishes.

Italian. Leading the fashionable band of Italian restaurants is **Orso**, 27 Wellington Street, Covent Garden, WC2 (tel: 071 240 5269), a large, fashionable and relatively pricey 1930s-style restaurant (sister of Joe Allen's) with a daily changing menu that includes pizzas and pasta. Open noon to midnight. **The River Café**, Thames Wharf, Rainville Road, W6 (tel: 071 385 3344), specialises in traditional farmhouse cooking (closed Saturday, lunch only on Sunday). **La Seppia** is a basement trattoria deep in the heart of Mayfair at 8a Mount Street, W1 (tel: 071 499 3385). Old-established fashionable favourites include the family run **San Martino**, 103 Walton Street, SW3 (tel: 071 589 3833), and **Santini**, 29 Ebury Street, SW1, near Victoria (tel: 071 730 4094), which has an elegant younger sister, **L'Incontro**, at 87 Pimlico Road, SW1 (tel: 071 730 6327). Other than that there are hundreds of 'fast-food' spaghetti and pizza restaurants.

and dance on the tables, while around the back of Bayswater, in Inverness Mews, there are two neighbouring 20-year-old branches of the taverna-like candlelit **Kalamaras** (tel: 071 727 9122): No 66 (unlicensed) and 76 (Greek wine and ouzo), both offering genuine Greek food (no pita and hummus). These provide meals during the evenings only (closed on Sunday). The proprietor sometimes plays on the bouzouki.

FOOD AND DRINK

Japanese. More reasonable than most are **Nanten Yakitori Bar**, 6 Blandford Street, W1 (tel: 071 935 6319), **Ginnan**, 5 Cathedral Place, EC4 in the City (tel: 071 236 4120) and **Ninjin**, 244 Great Portland Street, W1 (tel: 071 388 4657). All are part of the Ninjin group, who also have a Japanese restaurant in the Hilton International in Regent's Park and Kensington. Also worth trying is **Ikeda**, 30 Brook Street, W1 (tel: 071 499 7145), and the basement **Ikkyu**, 67 Tottenham Court Road, W1 (tel: 071 436 6169), with its excellent value set-meal lunches. Slightly more expensive, but with a cheaper set lunch, is **Miyama**, 38 Clarges Street, W1 (tel: 071 499 2443). Also see **Benihana**, Swiss Cottage, under Where to Eat with Children, page 104.

Jewish. **Bloom's**, 90 Whitechapel High Street, E1 (tel: 071 247 6001), serves chicken soup like mama makes. There is also a branch at 130 Golders Green Road, NW11 (tel: 071 455 1338).

Lebanese. **Al Hamra**, 31 Shepherd Market, W1 (tel: 071 493 1954), offers excellent Middle Eastern food. This fairly formal, busy restaurant (almost opposite the Curzon cinema), has an excellent selection of starters, hugh baskets of salads and raw vegetables on every table, and barbecued main courses. Less glamorous is **Maroush 1**, 21 Edgware Road, W2 (tel: 071 723 0773). The smarter **Maroush 11**, 38 Beauchamp Place, SW3 (tel: 071 581 5434), is near Harrods and is open until 4:30A.M.

Spanish. London has few Spanish restaurants of note.

Guernica, 21a Foley Street, W1 (tel: 071 580 0623) is an unnecessarily formal, fussy restaurant near Charlotte Street, specialising in Basque cuisine. If you want a genuine smoky *tapas* bar with a guitarist, try the **Meson don Felipe**, 53 The Cut, SE1, (tel: 071 928 3237) which is near the Old Vic theatre.

Thai. Several of the better Thai restaurants are in Soho. They include **Bahn Thai** , 21A Frith Street, W1 (tel: 071 437 8504), **Sri Siam**, 14 Old Compton Street, W1 (tel: 071 434 3544), and **Chiang Mai**, 48 Frith Street, W1 (tel: 071 437 7444). The **Blue Elephant**, at the far end of the Fulham Road in Fulham Broadway, is a fern-filled jungle (tel: 071 385 6595). By comparison, **Tui**, 19 Exhibition Road, SW7 (tel: 071 584 8359), is rather plain, but worth knowing about if you need a break from the nearby museums.

Pubs

People have stopped counting the 10,000-plus pubs in London and lost track of how old some of them are. Needless to say, several of Dickens' and Shakespeare's watering holes are historic enough to be included in sightseeing as well as drinking itineraries.

Don't expect too much in the way of home comforts in a London pub, though you may get a game of skittles or darts. The food is unlikely to be anything out of the ordinary either. However, if you want to sample a pork pie, a ploughman's (cheese and bread), bangers (sausages) and mash (potatoes), or shepherd's pie, a pub is the place to do it at a reasonable cost.

New licensing laws mean you can eat or drink all day, though some pubs still shut for a few hours in the afternoon. Closing time is generally 11:00P.M. (10:30P.M. on Sunday) though a handful of pubs, several down the Old Kent Road (tube: Elephant and Castle), stay open until 2.00A.M. If you want to take children the pub has to have a separate eating area. Several London pubs have live music and theatre.

The real test of any pub is the quality of its beer

The following pubs are reasonably central or on the river:

Bloomsbury and Holborn
The Lamb, 94 Lamb's Conduit Street, WC1. Small, intimate and friendly pub near Holborn, good for a snack lunch. Small courtyard and original 'snob screens'.
Museum Tavern, 49 Great Russell Street, WC1. Old-fashioned Victorian pub open all day, once frequented by Karl Marx and Virginia Woolf.

At lunchtime most pubs fill to bursting point

Princess Louise, 208 High Holborn, WC1. Popular with Londoners. Rather grand Victorian pub, with lots of polished mahogany, old tiles and brass. The 'gents' toilet is quite spectacular.

Chelsea
The Ferret and Firkin, Lots Road, SW10. Jolly pub with basic décor and a singalong piano or guitarist at night.
The Front Page, Old Church Street, SW3. Wealthy Chelsea resident's local. Good food.

Covent Garden
Lamb and Flag, 33 Rose Street, WC2. Low-ceilinged, 18th-century popular pub in an alley. Always packed.

Hampstead
The Holly Bush, Holly Mount, NW3. An 18th-century village

pub tucked away in a cobbled courtyard (opposite the station).

Kensington
The Anglesea Arms, Selwood Terrace, South Kensington, SW7. Early Victorian pub owned by Lady Joseph (Sir Maxwell's widow). Comfortable and civilized, with a terrace and open fire.
Windsor Castle, 114 Campden Hill Road, W8. Just off the Bayswater Road in Holland Park, an old-fashioned pub with good food and an open terrace garden. Popular in the evenings and on weekends.

Victoria
The Albert, Victoria Street, SW1. Victorian pub frequented by Members of Parliament. Division bell upstairs, huge staircase lined with portraits of Prime Ministers.

The River
(including the City and Docklands)
The Anchor, Bankside, SE1 (near Southwark Bridge). Dates back to 1750, the third inn on the site, with lots of little rooms and a terrace overlooking the river. Samuel Pepys, the 17th-century diarist, watched the Great Fire of London from here. On the tourist route.
The Angel, 101 Bermondsey Wall East, SE16. A 19th-century pub with fantastic views of Tower Bridge from the back gallery overhanging the river.
Dickens Inn, St Katharine's Yacht Haven, Docklands, E1. Very popular pub especially on weekends. Overlooks the boats and quayside entertainers, and has an open terrace and

exposed wooden beams and floorboards.
The Dove, 19 Upper Mall, Hammersmith, W6. Cosy, 17th-century riverside pub with tables and chairs outside. Near Ravenscourt Park or Stamford Brook tube.
George Inn, 77 High Street, Southwark, SE1 (near London Bridge Station). The only remaining galleried coaching inn in London, famous during the 18th and 19th centuries and mentioned by Dickens in *Little Dorrit*. Now run by the National Trust. You can sit outside in the cobbled courtyard. Occasional entertainment.
Horniman, Hays Galleria, SE1. Part of the new modern London Bridge City shopping development. On the Thames with views of HMS *Belfast* and Tower Bridge from the tables outside. Open all day.
Mayflower Inn, 117 Rotherhithe Street, SE16. On the Rotherhithe Walk through the Surrey Docks. The Pilgrim Fathers sailed from here and part of the pub dates back to the 16th century. Weekend barbecues.
Old Thameside, St Mary Wharf, Clink Street, SE1. New pub with a waterside setting between London and Blackfriars bridges, also champagne bar and riverside restaurant.
Prospect of Whitby, Wapping Wall, Docklands. Famous tavern with Tudor beams and flagstones. Live music nightly.
Samuel Pepys, High Timber Street, off 48 Upper Thames Street, EC4. Was a Victorian tea warehouse. Fine river views. There are two large bars and meals are served.

SHOPPING

SHOPPING

Opening Hours

Most shops are open from 9:00A.M. to 5:30P.M., with late-night opening until 8:00P.M. on Thursday in the West End and Kensington High Street and on Wednesday in Knightsbridge, King's Road and Sloane Square. Some Bond Street shops are shut all day or half day on Saturdays. Many shops in 'tourist areas' like Covent Garden and Tobacco Dock are open until 8:00P.M. nightly. Sunday opening laws are constantly under review, but you will find that some shops (not large stores) are open.

Sales

Prices get slashed at saletime. The winter sales start just before or after Christmas and run until early February. The summer sales begin in June or July and run through August. Look out for the last day of the sales in places like Harrods, where prices are reduced even further. Many of the larger stores have special mid-season sales.

VAT: See Money Matters section of Directory for relief from VAT for overseas visitors.

The Main Shopping Streets and Areas

There are enough shopping areas in London to fill a book on their own. Those below are the main areas.

The West End/Mayfair
Bond Street and South Molton Street

New Bond Street is synonymous with luxury. Once the home of Byron, Nelson and Beau Brummel, Bond Street begins at Oxford Street and runs south towards Piccadilly, becoming **Old Bond Street** about two-thirds of the way down. Once the most exclusive street in London, it is now more of a mixed bag, though it still offers high quality goods from silver to *haute couture*. Two famous landmarks are Sotheby's the auctioneers (Phillips' is in nearby Blenheim Street), and Asprey's for exquisite gifts. Fenwicks is good for accessories and women's

fashion, while the rather more exclusive White House specialises in linens as well as hand-embroidered clothes for children. You can buy sheet music in Chappell's, shoe shops include Rayne's (suppliers to the Royal family), and you'll find Cartier, Hermes, Chanel, Karl Lagerfeld, Ungaro and Ferragamo, and numerous antique shops, silversmiths and fine art galleries. Pedestrianised **South Molton Street** runs at an angle between Oxford Street and Brook Street which in turn leads into Bond Street. Here you will find several designer fashion outlets; Browns, Katherine Hamnett, Joseph Tricot, Kenzo and Bazaar among them, plus a few shoe shops and some selling costume jewellery. Café tables spill out onto the sidewalk in warm weather.

Looking for that special something?
Sotheby's might be the place for you

SHOPPING

Burlington Arcade, Savile Row and Cork Street

Burlington Arcade, built in 1819, and one of the last bastions of Edwardian London, runs parallel with Old Bond Street, north of Piccadilly and next to the Royal Academy. It is a covered, glass-domed arcade, lined with quality shops selling everything from antique jewellery to cashmere sweaters and Irish linen. Several are 'by Royal Appointment', and supply the Queen or other Royals.

Among the most tempting (running south from Burlington Gardens) are the Irish Linen Company, Christie (who specialise in bronze animals), Hummel (who do a good line in china dolls and tin soldiers) and Barrett and Co (whose window is full of almost priceless hand-painted miniature chess sets and Russian enamel jewellery). There is a branch of the herbalists Penhaligon's, several jewellers, and Zelli has an exquisite collection of fine porcelain.

If you are interested in art there are a number of galleries which are of interest, several contemporary, in and around **Cork Street** opposite. Turn left at the end, just past Gidden's of London saddlers, and you are in New Bond Street. Turn right if you want a hand-made suit from one of the exclusive tailors in the world-famous **Savile Row**.

Burlington Arcade. This is not the place to shop if you are on an economy drive

Chelsea

The main shopping area of Chelsea is the **King's Road**, which was originally the path Charles II took to visit Nell Gwyn in Fulham. Livelier than most other fashion areas, there are boutiques of every description, some of them selling whatever's currently in vogue second hand.

Kensington
A mixed area that includes **Kensington High Street** (department stores and boutiques), **Kensington Church Street** (antique shops), **Portobello Road** antique market, and the tiny newly fashionable **Brompton Cross**, round the corner from Harrods, with the Conran shop and Joseph's.

Knightsbridge
Knightsbridge is one of the most exclusive shopping areas. Harrods and Harvey Nichols at the top of **Sloane Street** are the two main stores, but you'll also find the Scotch House and an Emporio Armani just before you reach **Beauchamp Place**. There are numerous designer boutiques selling fashion and jewellery, and a long line of some of the most stylish designer shops in London leads south down Sloane Street.

Oxford Street
Nearly a mile long, full of cheap fashion shops and chain stores, interspersed with good-value department stores: Marks & Spencer, Selfridges, C&A, House of Fraser, John Lewis, Debenhams, Littlewoods and British Home Stores. Private cars are not allowed in parts of Oxford Street, but even the widened sidewalks haven't eased congestion. Illegal marketeers attract crowds that clog up the sidewalks (their cheap perfumes will probably be water, so watch out). Round the back of Selfridges, the pedestrianised **St Christopher's Place** offers quality fashion boutiques and a bit of peace and quiet.

Covent Garden
A fashionable area that attracts young people and visitors. Shops are clustered around the covered central market building, with antiques and crafts sold from the original wrought-iron trading stands. The area is very expensive.

SHOPPING

Austin Reed – famous for men's clothes

Piccadilly and St James's

Piccadilly is a busy thoroughfare with airline offices and car showrooms either side of the Ritz and the Royal Academy of Arts. It has old-fashioned shopping arcades (including Burlington Arcade) selling everything from luggage to crystal, Fortnum and Mason, with its exotic food hall, Simpson for clothes and Hatchards for books. Beyond Piccadilly are the indoor shopping complexes of the Trocadero and London Pavillion while in the **Haymarket**, Burberrys sell the famous trenchcoats.

Jermyn Street, south of Piccadilly in St James's, is unashamedly old fashioned and male orientated, offering hand-made shirts and shoes, Havana cigars, antiques, fine art and antique scientific instruments. There is also Floris, perfumiers to the Court of St James since George IV, and half-way along is Fortnum's Fountain Restaurant and a branch of Dunhill's for gifts.

Regent Street and Carnaby Street

Regent Street curves down from Oxford Circus to Piccadilly. Designed by John Nash, it houses some impressive buildings including the mock-Tudor façade of Liberty's department store. There are several airline offices, Dickins and Jones department store, a branch of Laura Ashley, Hamleys' toyshop and several shops selling china and crystal, plus the Queen's jewellers, Garrard. Shops specialising in classic British fashion include Jaeger, Austin Reed and Aquascutum. Round the back is the pedestrianised **Carnaby Street**. This used to be *the* street to be seen in during the 1960s, but now you should avoid it unless you like tourist junk.

Soho

Soho is changing fast but there are still long-established family firms, selling Continental food, coffee, cigars or cakes, though they may soon be pushed out by property developers and high rents as the area becomes even more desirable. The inevitable replacements are boutiques, bars and restaurants. **Gerrard Street** caters to its Chinese community and there is a lively fruit and vegetable market in **Berwick Street**.

Tobacco Dock

London's newest shopping centre in Docklands (opened in the spring of 1989) is twice the size of Covent Garden, with over 100 shops (open until 8:00P.M.) and restaurants housed in a grade one listed Georgian building off the Highway. To get there take the East London Underground to Wapping, or Docklands Light Railway from Tower Gateway (Bank from summer 1991) to Shadwell, then follow the signposted directions.

Markets

London's market traders are a dying breed as the main wholesale markets get squeezed out of the capital by redevelopment. Covent Garden's fruit and vegetable traders are now in Nine Elms, Billingsgate fish market has moved to West India Dock, and Spitalfields' future is in doubt as the area is set to be developed as an international banking centre.

At the turn of the century there were some 60,000 street sellers, called 'costers', hawking anything they could get their hands on in a desperate attempt to earn a living. The markets of the East End were full of Romany fortune tellers, quack doctors and organ grinders. Food stalls sold pies and eels. You could get your shoes blacked or your knives sharpened. Illegal traders carted off half the food to be sold in poorer districts, talking in rhyming slang (*eg* 'apples and pears'; stairs) to fool the police. Today the street markets that are left sell fruit, sometimes of dubious quality unless you know the stallholder, second-hand clothes, and rubbish that's 'fallen off the back of a truck'. Antiques at largely inflated prices are sold off stalls in Portobello Road, but if you get up early enough there are bargains to be had at the New Caledonian Market on a Friday morning in Bermondsey. As for the old 'costers', they're still around in the East End, dressing up in their finest costumes as 'pearly Kings and Queens' for special occasions like the Lord Mayor's Show.

The following markets are still going strong:

Antiques
Camden Passage, off Upper Street, Islington, N1 (tube: Angel). Individual stalls on Wednesdays (6:45A.M. to 4:00P.M.) and Saturdays (8:00A.M. to 5:00P.M.), also Thursday for prints and drawings; quality shops open all week in adjoining streets.
New Caledonian Market, Bermondsey Square, SE1 (tube: London Bridge). Huge open-air market from 6:00A.M. to 2:00P.M. on Fridays. Trade plus anyone else who gets there early enough. Lots of jewellery. **Portobello Road**, W11 (tube: Notting Hill Gate, Ladbroke Grove). The antique-stall holders turn up from 7:00A.M. to 5:00P.M. on Saturdays, though a lot of the prices are inflated for visitors. Shops and arcades are also worth visiting.

Other Goods
Brick Lane, E1 (tube: Aldgate East). East End market. Sunday 5:00A.M. to 2:00P.M.. Lots of rock-bottom rubbish. A good place for a decent bagel.
Camden Lock, Camden Town, NW1 (tube: Chalk Farm, Camden Town). Several small markets, with crafts and jewellery sold under awnings in the crowded Lock area at the weekends (8:00A.M. to 6:00P.M.), when most of

the local shops (prints, furniture etc) are also open. Undergoing redevelopment. Fruit and vegetables are sold in Inverness Street daily, there's a small antique market in Camden High Street on Thursdays and weekends and more bric-à-brac in the **Chalk Farm** market down the road.

Covent Garden, WC2 (tube: Covent Garden). Crafts and mostly British-made goods are sold on weekdays and weekends, with antiques on Mondays. Spills over into the more general Jubilee Market to the south of the piazza. 9:00A.M. to 5:00P.M.

A stall in Camden Passage

SHOPPING

Petticoat Lane. Some stallholders have turned the business of attracting bored shoppers into an art form

Greenwich Market, Greenwich High Road, SE10 (British Rail: Greenwich). Weekend market (better on sunday) selling antiques, crafts and second-hand clothes. 7:00A.M. to 5:30P.M.
Leather Lane, EC1 (tube: Chancery Lane). A bit of everything from cheap silk ties to cassettes, woolly sweaters to palm trees. Monday to Friday 10:00A.M. to 2:30P.M.
Petticoat Lane, Middlesex Street, E1 (tube: Aldgate or Aldgate East). Don't look for Petticoat Lane itself because you won't find it. Sunday is the day for clothes. Try Goulston Street at the far end for designer clothes. Brick Lane specialises in electrical goods and furniture. 9:00A.M. to 2:00P.M., Sunday.

ACCOMMODATION

Nearly a quarter of all visitors to London stay with friends or relatives. For the rest the London Tourist Board produces two guides: *Where to Stay in London*, which covers hotels, b&b, guesthouses and apartments, and *London Budget Hotels*. They also have a separate leaflet, *Accommodation For Families*. The AA (British Automobile Association) also publishes several guides to London.

The London Tourist Board can book accommodation if you call in at their office at Victoria Station or Heathrow on arrival, or you can write to them at 26 Grosvenor Gardens, London, SW1W 0DU, at least six weeks in advance of your visit. Alternatively, telephone 071 824 8844. (Access or Visa required.) A deposit and communication charge is payable when making a reservation.

Apartments

There are numerous agencies dealing with short-term apartment rentals (usually a minimum of one week). You can get a list from the London Tourist Board. Agencies include:
AAE Ltd (tel: 071 794 1186)
Accommodation in London (tel: 071 224 3630)
Holiday Flat Services Ltd (tel: 071 486 8646)
London's universities and colleges make their halls of residence available to visitors at Easter and from July to September. To make reservations telephone 071 636 2818.

Bed and Breakfast

The London Tourist Board lists b&b hotels (see Hotels) as well as agencies that will find you accommodation with a private family. Many of the private homes are in the suburbs and you have no guarantee that you will be included in family life. You may or may not get the option of an evening meal, or a packed lunch, and there may be a minimum stay.

The b&b agencies for accommodation in private homes include:
Anglo World Travel (tel: 071 387 9441)
Capital Homes (tel: 071 440 7535)
Home Stay (tel: 071 641 2548)
London Homestead Services (tel: 071 602 1334)
London Visitor Accommodation Bureau (tel: 081 440 0857)
World Wide Bed and Breakfast Association (tel: 071 370 7099)

Hotels

London hotels are notoriously expensive although most also offer corporate rates and attractively priced weekend breaks. Some hotels offer free accommodation to children sharing your room. Don't hesitate to ask either a travel agent or the hotel itself about bargain breaks; even the most exclusive establishments like the Ritz, the Savoy and the Hyatt Carlton Tower offer them. The following agencies will make hotel reservations for you:
British Hotel Reservation Centre toll free (tel: 0800 282888)
Concordia-Worldwide Hotel Reservations (tel: 071 730 3467)
Hotel Booking Service (tel: 071 437 5052)
Hotelguide (tel: 071 836 5561)
The Leading Hotels of the World (toll free) (tel: 0800 181123)

ACCOMMODATION

Prestige (toll free) (tel: 0800 282124)
Room Centre (UK) (tel: 071 328 1790)
Hotels are officially classified by a 'listed' or crown system from one to five. Those that display the crown have met certain criteria and have been inspected. Given here is a selection of London hotels in a variety of locations divided up according to price.

Very Expensive

The most exclusive hotels in the capital are in Piccadilly, Mayfair and Knightsbridge. The **Ritz** in Piccadilly (tel: 071 493 8181) opened in 1906 and soon became one of the most fashionable hotels in the world, frequented by Royalty and celebrities from Noël Coward to the Aga Khan. (The latter had a suite there for over 40 years.) If your finances don't run to staying there you can (if you book ahead) have tea in the Palm Court. The sumptuous **Dorchester** in Park Lane (tel: 071 629 8888) has now reopened its doors after extensive refurbishment and is also one of the world's ultimate luxury hotels. The rather less flamboyant **Athenaeum** (tel: 071 499 3464) near Hyde Park Corner, overlooks Green Park. The Savoy Group includes the Savoy, the Connaught, Claridge's and the Berkeley. The **Connaught** in Carlos Place, Mayfair (tel: 071 499 7070) was created as a London home for the landed gentry. The staff wear morning dress and it feels more like a country house than a hotel. **Claridge's** (tel: 071 629 8860) in Brook Street opened its doors in

The Connaught – judged the best hotel in Europe, by the AA in 1988

1899. You may be welcomed by a Hungarian Quartet. Royalty often drop in for lunch in the Causerie. The **Savoy** (tel: 071 836 4343) in the Strand recently celebrated its centenary and its standards are still exemplary. At the turn of the

Knightsbridge, where the General Manager is from the Grand in Rome. It has wonderful views over the park from the rear, and with £2 million worth of renovations the Hyde Park Hotel hopes to become THF's flagship in London by the time it celebrates its centenary in 1992. If you like to work out or have a swim, the **Grosvenor House** (tel: 071 499 6363) in Park Lane has an attractive indoor pool, as does the **Berkeley** in Wilton Place, Belgravia (tel: 071 235 6000) where the sliding lid of the rooftop is removed in summer. **Le Meridien** in Piccadilly (tel: 071 734 8000) has a Champneys health club with a superb Roman-style pool complete with Grecian statues, and the **Hyatt Carlton Tower** in Cadogan Place off Sloane Street (tel: 071 235 5411) has a ninth and tenth floor gym and fitness club, The Peak, which also offers views over Knightsbridge.
Overlooking Hyde Park, the **Inter-Continental** (tel: 071 409 3131) and the **Inn on the Park** (tel: 071 499 0888) both cater well to businessmen. The Inter-Continental has a fitness centre. At the Inn on the Park the second-floor suites have conservatories. Both hotels have excellent restaurants.

Small Hotels
London's smaller hotels are often converted out of terraced houses, and furnished more like a home than a hotel. Among the best are:
The Capital in Basil Street near Harrods (tel: 071 589 5171); the pretty, chintzy **Halcyon** on the corner of Holland Park and Holland Park Avenue, with its

century it was so popular with Royalty that the special bell that heralded their arrival was abandoned. There are splendid river views from the highly acclaimed restaurant, and an American Bar.
Italians will feel quite at home at the **Hyde Park Hotel** (tel: 071 235 2000) opposite Harvey Nichols in

ACCOMMODATION

fashionable Kingfisher garden restaurant (tel: 071 727 7288); the stylish **Blakes Hotel** owned by the celebrated Anouska Hempel in Roland Gardens, South Kensington (tel: 071 370 6701); and tiny **Dukes** in a cobbled alley behind St James's (tel: 071 491 4840) and the neighbouring **Stafford** (tel: 071 493 0111), both with excellent restaurants. **Browns** (tel: 071 493 6020) started off small enough when it opened in 1837, but now occupies 14 elegant town houses in Albemarle and Dover Streets off Bond Street, while the **Chesterfield** in Charles Street, Mayfair (tel: 071 491 2622), was once the home of the 4th Earl of Chesterfield.

Expensive enough:
The **Goring** in Beeston Place (tel: 071 834 8211), near Buckingham Palace, has been going strong since 1910 and is still owned by the original family. **L'Hôtel** in Basil Street (tel: 071 589 6286) is essentially a b&b establishment but wonderfully central. For lovers of antiques the **Portobello Hotel** in Stanley Gardens (tel: 071 727 2777) is near the market of that name. For river views try the modern **Tower Thistle Hotel** in St Katharine's Way (tel: 071 481 2575), or the slightly more expensive **Royal Horseguards Thistle** in Whitehall Court (tel: 071 839 3400). There are six Hiltons in London, including the modern **Hilton International Regent's Park** (tel: 071 722 7722) in St John's Wood, which just about overlooks Lord's cricket ground and has a good Japanese restaurant and New York deli, and the **London Hilton Mews**

One of the bedrooms in Holland Park's Halcyon Hotel

Hotel (tel: 071 493 7222) in Stanhope Row, behind the **London Hilton on Park Lane** (tel: 071 493 8000) which has splendid views of London from its high-rise windows in Park Lane.

Small Hotels
If you prefer a more personal atmosphere, the 28-roomed **Beaufort Hotel** (b&b and light snacks only) in peaceful Beaufort Gardens, near Harrods (tel: 071

584 5252) is a town house that gives guests their own front-door key. The Regency-style **Dorset Square Hotel** (tel: 071 723 7874) near Regent's Park is hot on chintzes and beautiful fabrics. The b&b only **Fenja**, 69 Cadogan Gardens near Sloane Square (tel: 071 589 7333), is a member of the Prestige group and is decorated with fine antiques and English Masters. You wouldn't know that **11 Cadogan Gardens** (tel: 071 730 3426) was a hotel at all; four Victorian town houses (60 rooms) have been converted into an

elegant hotel furnished with antiques and paintings. Regular visitors include diplomats and art dealers. It offers 24-hour room service with light meals.

Reasonable:

One of London's best b&b hotels and a winner of awards is the **Claverley** in Beaufort Gardens, a few minutes from Harrods (tel: 071 589 8541). The **Pembridge Court**, a Victorian town house near Portobello Road, in Pembridge Gardens (tel: 071 229 9977), has only 26 rooms and its

ACCOMMODATION

own restaurant. Handy for Victoria Station is the b&b only **Elizabeth Hotel** in Eccleston Square (tel: 071 828 6812), as is the **Ebury Court** (tel: 071 730 8147), with accommodation in five adjoining houses. Similarly converted out of three terraced houses is **Hazlitt's** in Frith Street in Soho (tel: 071 434 1771). North of Oxford Street, **Durrants Hotel** (tel: 071 935 8131) in George Street near Baker Street is one of the oldest privately owned hotels in London. Reasonably priced for Knightsbridge is the recently renovated **Knightsbridge Green Hotel** which is near Harrods (tel: 071 584 6274).

If you don't mind staying in North London, both the **Swiss Cottage Hotel** in Adamson Road (tel: 071 722 2281), and the **Sandringham** in Holford Road near Hampstead Heath (tel: 071 435 1569), offer b&b in a quiet location and have been converted out of Victorian houses. The West End is a bus ride or a few stops away on the tube, and the areas in which the hotels are set are themselves worth exploring.

Quiet and unobtrusive; the Sandringham Hotel at Hampstead

ENTERTAINMENT

There is always an enormous choice of what to see in London, most of it in the West End or just across Waterloo Bridge in the rather ugly concrete South Bank Arts Centre. Opened in 1976, the latter is long overdue for a facelift. Alongside the National Theatre and Hayward Gallery is the Royal Festival Hall, built in 1951 for the Festival of Britain. The neighbouring Queen Elizabeth Hall and the Purcell Room were opened in 1967. The Barbican, in the City is home to the Royal Shakespeare Company and London Symphony Orchestras and is a major venue for art exhibitions and concerts. The Royal Opera and Royal Ballet perform at the Royal Opera House and the English National Opera at the Coliseum. London's newest venue is the $35 million London Arena, a modern building at Limeharbour on the Isle of Dogs. It can seat 12,000 people and offers everything from sports to classical concerts and exhibitions. Dress is fairly informal for concerts and the theatre, but most people dress up for the Royal Opera House. Theatres tend to be hot and stuffy, and although you can leave coats in cloakrooms, lines tend to be long, so a light coat you can fold up and put on your lap is the best idea. During intermission, bars sell drinks (you can order in advance) and light snacks.

Clubs/Discos

It is not worth listing whats 'in', because it probably won't be by next week! Needless to say, most clubs are for members only. If you are staying at a top hotel the concierge may be able to get you into a nightclub like **Annabel's** for the evening. If you happen to have media friends in the capital you could be taken for a drink on a comfortable sofa or a meal at Groucho's in Soho. Trendy young Londoners belong to Fred's or Moscow's. But you have to know a member to get in. If you're from out of town and punk, funk, yuppie, or anything else, the best you can do is to buy the weekly *Time Out* magazine and look up the clubs (that don't need membership) currently in vogue. The **Hippodrome**, Charing Cross Road, WC2 (tel: 071 437 4311) is where to go for dancing. It's central, loud and expensive, with hi-tech décor and the best lasers in town. **Stringfellow's**, 16 Upper St Martin's Lane, WC2 (tel: 071 240 5534) is rather more intimate and sophisticated and you can also eat there.

You can eat or drink, listen to music, live blues, jazz or soul and dance at the **Dover Street Wine Bar**, 8–9 Dover Street, W1 (tel: 071 629 9813), until 3:00 A.M. every day but Sunday.

Jazz

London has few central jazz venues compared to other capitals, but it does have some informal venues in pubs and restaurants. A selection is listed below.

The Bass Clef, 35 Coronet Street, off Hoxton Square, N1 (tel: 071 729 2476). Serious venue for young artists who perform on a stage in a dim cellar. Cheap food.
The 100 Club, 100 Oxford Street,

W1 (tel: 071 636 0933). A small smoky basement which offers jazz and blues nights with Caribbean food; live music.
Ronnie Scott's, 47 Frith Street, W1 (tel: 071 439 0747). In the heart of Soho, this is London's most sophisticated jazz club, dimly lit and smoky, with regularly changing acts of international status. You can eat here but it is expensive. Reservations essential for the most popular artists. Closed Sunday.

Restaurants with live jazz include:
Pizza Express, 10 Dean Street, W1 (tel: 071 437 9595). Jazz basement.
Pizza on the Park 11–13 Knightsbridge, SW1 (tel. 071 235 5550). Near Hyde Park Corner. Live music every night in separate basement jazz room.

Concerts/Classical Music
Concerts and classical music are performed at numerous venues. If you are in London during the summer, the **Henry Wood Promenade Concerts** (or Proms), held from the end of July in the red-brick Royal Albert Hall, are great fun, but lines for the standing area in the body of the hall can form early on in the day. The main classical music venues are:
The Barbican Hall, Silk Street, EC2 (tel: 071 638 8891)
London Arena, Limeharbour, E14 (tel: 071 538 1212)
Purcell Room, South Bank, SE1 (tel: 071 928 8800)
Queen Elizabeth Hall, South Bank, SE1 (tel: 071 928 8800)
Royal Albert Hall, Kensington Gore, SW7 (tel: 071 589 3203)
Royal Festival Hall, South Bank,

The Royal Opera House has been the setting for many memorable operatic evenings

SE1 (tel: 071 928 8800)
Wigmore Hall, Wigmore Street, W1 (tel: 071 935 2141)
Free concerts take place in the foyers of the Barbican and the National Theatre on the South Bank, on weekends and early in the evening. Free lunchtime concerts of organ music, string quartets, piano recitals, brass bands etc are held in churches, many of them in the City.

Dance

The Royal Ballet performs at the **Royal Opera House** in Covent Garden. In summer the English National Opera moves out of the **Coliseum** to make room for major ballet companies, while the London Contemporary Dance School as well as touring companies give performances at **The Place**. There are also major performances at **Sadler's Wells** in Islington and in the South Bank concert halls (see listings above.) Addresses and phone numbers are:

London Coliseum, St Martin's Lane, WC2 (tel: 071 836 3161)
The Place, 17 Duke's Road, WC1 (tel: 071 387 0031)
Royal Opera House, Covent Garden, WC2 (tel: 071 240 1066)
Sadler's Wells, Rosebery Avenue, EC1 (tel: 071 278 8916)

Opera

The first opera at the **Royal Opera House**, in Covent Garden, was performed in 1817 and they've been playing to packed houses ever since. If you can't afford a dress circle seat

ENTERTAINMENT

(very expensive) you can always sneak into the famous 'crush bar' during intermission to soak up the atmosphere. If you're lucky your visit may coincide with the odd summer night when a huge screen is erected and sound relayed into the Covent Garden piazza outside.

Prices are a lot cheaper and the operas are sung in English at the English National Opera's home at the **Coliseum**. Operas are also occasionally performed at other venues including the concert halls on the South Bank.
English National Opera, The London Coliseum, St Martin's Lane, WC2 (tel: 071 836 3161)
Royal Opera House, Covent Garden, WC2 (tel: 071 240 1066)

Theatre

Most London theatres are in and around Soho and Covent Garden. The **National Theatre** and the **Old Vic** are across Waterloo Bridge on the South Bank, the **Barbican** is in the City. There are also numerous small repertory or 'fringe' theatres all over London (see below). Performances usually begin at 7:30 or 8:00P.M. with matinées often on Wednesday and Saturday afternoons. Theatres are closed on Sundays. If your visit coincides with Christmas you'll find that many theatres offer a traditional pantomime, while in the summer you can watch a Shakespearean play in the delightful open-air setting of Regent's Park.

Fringe Theatre. London has an enormous network of fringe theatres extending into the suburbs both north and south of the river. Performances are highly regarded, though companies are often ill-funded and perform on a shoe-string. Many take place in pub theatres, some at lunchtime. The most well-known venues include:
The Almeida, Almeida Street, N1 (tel: 071 359 4404)
Donmar Warehouse, 41 Earlham Street, WC2 (tel: 071 240 8230)
ICA Theatre, The Mall, W1 (tel: 071 930 3647); King's Head, Upper Street, N1 (tel: 071 226 8561)
Riverside Studios, Crisp Road, W6 (tel: 081 748 3354)
Be prepared for uncomfortable seats, and minimal scenery. There is no need to dress up. Admission charges are low and you usually have to become a member for a small charge which you can do at the door. For more information contact The Pub Theatre Network (tel: 071 835 1853) or see *Time Out*.

Tickets

To get tickets for shows and theatre you should use a reputable ticket agency (see **Directory**). The box offices of the individual theatres are usually open from 10:00A.M. to 8:00P.M. and you can book over the telephone by credit card (picking up your tickets just before the performance), or go along in person. You may also be lucky if you line up for returns on the day. Seats for West End shows aren't cheap. The National Theatre is more reasonable.
For half-price tickets (to theatres and sometimes for the English National Opera) go in person on the day to the blue and red SWET ticket booth in Leicester Square. There is a small booking fee, and payment is by cash only.

If you want bargain theatre tickets, the Leicester Square Ticket Booth is the place for you

The booth is open from Monday to Saturday from noon until half an hour before the matinée performances and from 2:30P.M. to 6:30P.M. for evening shows. Up to four tickets per person.

What's On

You can find out what's on from any of the quality daily or Sunday newspapers, or, with more lengthy (and fairly radical) reviews, in the weekly *Time Out* magazine.

Tourist Offices (see **Directory**) will also have information on entertainment in the capital.

WEATHER AND WHEN TO GO

Whenever you choose to travel to London, pack an umbrella and a light raincoat. In the last few years London's weather seems to have become totally unpredictable. There have been crocuses in bloom in February, the worst storms in memory in October, incessant rain in normally dry months, plus little summer to speak of. Traditionally the wettest month is November. July and August are also wet, but the average daily maximum temperatures reach 71 degrees Fahrenheit (22 degrees Centigrade). March and April are the driest months, despite what you may have heard about April showers. You may get snow in winter, but you cannot bank on it.

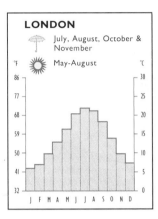

LONDON

July, August, October & November

May–August

To listen to a recorded weather forecast for the London area phone 0898 500401.

Whatever the season, a military band might appear from nowhere to entertain the crowds

HOW TO BE A LOCAL

'Londoners' are hard to define. Cockneys refuse to extend the description to anyone not born within the sound of Bow Bells. North Londoners scoff at South Londoners' claims to be locals, and vice versa. In fact, most Londoners are not really Londoners in any strict sense. It's a diverse, cosmopolitan city – but there are plenty of ways to tell a 'local' from a tourist. Londoners are always in a hurry. If you feel ignored, don't be offended; they don't talk to each other in public, let alone strangers.

Londoners don't go to the 'historic' pubs on the Thames unless they are next door to the office, and when a publican calls 'time gentlemen, please', Londoners have already ordered their last drinks.

At lunchtime (noon to 2:00P.M.) the pubs are bursting, so if you can, visit them outside these hours. All the sandwich bars will also be full to overflowing, so buy your sandwiches before the rush begins. Londoners who want to eat their lunch in comparative peace go to the parks; those who are really in the know go to the Inns of Court or to the Temple, where the squares have never emerged into the 20th century. These are excellent places to get away from London's dreadful traffic (pollution from exhaust is a genuine cause of fear these days).

In shops, Londoners know better than to expect the salesperson to offer much in the way of help and accept that purchases will be crumpled up and shoved into a plastic bag.

Londoners who can, avoid supermarkets and West End shops on a Saturday morning. They know that it's much easier to park (and the meters are free) on Saturday afternoon. They never drive into town without plenty of change for meters and don't expect to get their windshield washed when they fill up with gas.

If they go to museums it's with the children during vacations or on a Sunday afternoon, they always eat before they go because they know the cafés will be full. Londoners over 30 wait for new films to come to their local cinema and rarely venture into the West End on a Saturday night except to see a play. They know better than to try to get into a decent film, play or restaurant without reservations.

Many of the most exciting plays are staged outside the West End anyway, in alternative venues – such as rooms above pubs. Look for these and every other form of entertainment in the weekly magazine *Time Out*.

Londoners hate travelling by public transport. They resign themselves to long waits at bus stops followed by the sudden arrival of a convoy of buses all for the same route.

They know that the tubes will be horribly overcrowded during the rush hour (8:00 to 9:30A.M. and 4:30 to 6:30P.M.) and they also know that delays are likely at any time. As for the railway network, well, it brings many commuters close to tears on a regular basis and that's the only reliable thing about it.

Londoners like to describe the city as a series of villages, and

HOW TO BE A LOCAL

enjoy having 'their own' shops and parks, off the beaten track. If they want to go for a walk in the City, they go on Sundays, when the whole of the 'square mile' is virtually deserted. To buy trendy clothes they go to Camden Market and this is also where you can go to see the colourful and eccentric side of London.

Despite their generally grim outlook, Londoners love processions, festivals, marches, demonstrations and anything else that could be described as a 'bit of a do' (it really is true about the use of understatement, by the way).

Derby Day at Epsom. This is one of the great events in the British racing calendar

SPECIAL EVENTS

The London Tourist Board produces a leaflet on events. Some of those that take place on an annual basis are listed below. Exact dates vary from year to year.

January

Lord Mayor of Westminster's New Year's Day Parade.

Marching bands, dancers and performers parade from Piccadilly to Hyde Park, culminating in a firework display.

February

Gun Salute on Accession Day (6th; day after if Sunday) 41-gun salute (noon) opposite the Dorchester Hotel in Hyde Park. Cruft's Dog Show at Earl's Court.

March

The Oxford versus Cambridge University Boat Race, from Putney to Mortlake.

April

Easter Parade (sometimes in March, depending on when Easter falls) in Battersea Park on Easter Sunday, followed by the Harness Parade Horse in the Inner Circle of Regent's Park on Easter Monday.
Gun Salute on the Queen's Birthday (21st).

May

Chelsea Flower Show in the Chelsea Royal Hospital Grounds. Some days open to members only.
FA Cup Final, Wembley. For soccer fans.

June

Beating the Retreat: Household Division, Horse Guards Parade, SW1. Military display of marching and drilling bands with massed bands and pipers. Also evening performances.
Derby Day. Epsom's famous race for three-year-old colts and fillies.
Royal Academy Summer Exhibition. Royal Academy of Arts, Piccadilly (until mid-August).
Stella Artois Tennis

SPECIAL EVENTS

Bright young things at Henley. The Regatta always attracts leisurely crowds

Championships, Queen's Club, W14.

Beating the Retreat. Tri-Service Massed Bands, Horse Guards Parade, SW1.

Queen's Official Birthday (Saturday, mid-June).

Trooping the Colour. Parade leaves Buckingham Palace at 10:40A.M. and travels down The Mall to Horse Guards Parade, arriving at 11:00A.M.. Return to Buckingham Palace with flyby by the RAF and appearance on the balcony at 1:00P.M. with another gun salute at the Tower of London.

Royal Ascot, Ascot Racecourse, Berkshire. The Queen and the Royal family attend the famous races. Starts at 2:30P.M. each day. Formal attire and a hat essential.

Wimbledon Lawn Tennis Championships, All England Club, Wimbledon, SW19. Late June to early July. Tickets for centre courts need booking well in advance.

Henley Royal Regatta, Henley-on-Thames, Oxfordshire. Late June to early July. International rowing regatta held since 1839.

July

Royal Tournament, Earl's Court, SW5. Spectacular by the Armed Forces in aid of service charities. Much pomp and pageantry, and attended by the Royal Family. Henry Wood Promenade concerts, the Proms (informal jazz to symphonic), held at the Royal Albert Hall. Mid-July to Mid-September. The last night is the most riotous.

Swan Upping. A traditional ceremony to 'mark' the swans and record their numbers. Takes place on the Thames from Sunbury to Whitchurch (3rd week of July).

August

London Riding Horse Parade, Rotten Row, Hyde Park. A competition to choose the best turned out horse and rider. Notting Hill Carnival. Held over the Late Summer Holiday weekend in the streets of Notting Hill and Ladbroke Grove. A usually peaceful Caribbean-style procession and party with steel bands, dancing in the streets and lots of loud reggae until 9:00A.M., with costume competitions at noon.

September

Horseman's Sunday. Church service conducted by a vicar on horseback at Church of St John and St Michael, Hyde Park Crescent, W2. Horses assemble at 11:30A.M.. Ends 1:00P.M. then horses go on a procession through Hyde Park.

October

Pearly Harvest Festival Service, held at 3:00P.M. at St Martin-in-the-Fields, WC2, attended by London's Pearly Kings and Queens (the traditional cockney costermongers).

Judges Service. Opening of the legal year on the first weekday in October, with judges in full ceremonial robes. 11:00A.M. at Westminster Abbey. View the procession from Westminster Abbey to the Houses of Parliament at 11:45A.M.

Trafalgar Day Parade to celebrate Nelson's victory. Held in Trafalgar Square on the nearest Sunday to the 21st.

November

Guy Fawkes Night (5th). His attempt to blow up Parliament in 1605 is commemorated by bonfires and fireworks. London to Brighton Veteran Car Run. Held on the first Sunday in November. Several hundred entrants and their pride and joys in gleaming condition leave Hyde Park Corner early in the morning and take the A23 to Brighton.

Lord Mayor's Show. Takes place on a Saturday in mid-November. The Lord Mayor rides in his gilded coach to the Law Courts for the declaration of office. Colourful floats and military bands start at around 11:00A.M. from Gresham Street for Mansion House, passing St Paul's, Fleet Street and the Strand.

State Opening of Parliament. Mid-November. The Royal Procession travels along The Mall, through Horse Guards Parade. Departs at 11:00A.M.

Christmas Lights. Switched on in Oxford Street, Regent Street and Bond Street from mid-November until early January.

CHILDREN

There is no accounting for children's taste. Some like museums, others hate them. The boredom factor may be alleviated by the quiz sheets provided by some of the major museums and galleries, and there are often special events, or films, either on weekends or during the holidays. If you have children who like 'doing things', both the Launch Pad at the Science Museum and the Human Biology Hall at the Natural History Museum will provide hours of educationally interactive fun for all ages. Children are charged half-price admission in museums and under 5's usually get in free. There are also numerous other possibilities, from cinemas and theatres that put on children's films and plays, to puppet shows and parks. Babysitters can be arranged via Childminders (tel: 071 935 9763) or Universal Aunts (tel: 071 351 5767).

One of the most useful sources of up-to-the-minute information is Capital Radio's *London for Kids* magazine (from good bookshops), or the children's section of *Time Out* magazine (available from newsagents).

For details of children's clubs, classes, sports and holiday entertainment, call Kidsline (tel: 071 222 8070), weekdays 9:00A.M. to 4:00P.M. during school vacations, 4:00P.M. to 6:00P.M. during the term.

The following should provide something of interest for most age groups (see pages 25–42 for further details).

HMS *Belfast*, London Bridge

Try it yourself – the Science Museum's Launch Pad

British Museum, Bloomsbury,
Buckingham Palace (and the Changing of the Guard every morning in summer and alternate mornings in winter at 11:30A.M., also at Horse Guards in Whitehall)
Cutty Sark, Greenwich
Guinness World of Records, Piccadilly
Hampton Court Palace (and the maze), Hampton Court
Horniman Museum, Forest Hill

London Brass Rubbing Centre, Trafalgar Square
London Transport Museum, Covent Garden
Madame Tussaud's, Marylebone
Museum of the Moving Image, South Bank
Natural History Museum, South Kensington
Planetarium, Marylebone
Rock Circus, Piccadilly
Science Museum, South Kensington
Thames Barrier, Woolwich
Tower of London, City

Other places of interest for children include:

◆◆
BETHNEL GREEN MUSEUM OF CHILDHOOD
Cambridge Heath Road, E2
A branch of the Victoria and Albert devoted to what man has made for children, with toys through the centuries, dolls and doll's houses, puppets, children's dress and nursery furniture. Saturday workshops in the art room at 11:00A.M. and 2:00P.M.

CHILDREN

In the garden of the London Toy and Model Museum

Holiday activities. Free.
Open: Monday to Thursday and Saturday 10:00A.M. to 6:00P.M., Sunday 2:30P.M. to 6:00P.M.; closed Fridays
Tube: Bethnal Green (next door)

◆
COMMONWEALTH INSTITUTE
Kensington High Street, W8
Often over-looked is the Centre for Commonwealth education and culture in Britain with changing exhibitions reflecting the people and issues of some 48 countries. Festivals, workshops and holiday activities. Free.

Open: 10:00A.M. to 5:00P.M., Sunday 2:00P.M. to 5:00P.M.
Tube: High Street Kensington

◆
DICKENS' HOUSE
48 Doughty Street, near Gray's Inn Road, WC1
A museum since 1925. The house where Dickens lived and where he wrote his first full-length novel, *The Pickwick Papers*, and later *Oliver Twist* and *Nicholas Nickelby*. Displays include from 1837 to 1839 manuscripts, furniture, letters, first editions and period rooms.
Open: daily 10:00A.M. to 5:00P.M.; closed Sundays
Tube: Russell Square, Chancery Lane

♦
GEFFREYE MUSEUM
136 Kingsland Road, E2
Collection of period furniture
from 1600 to 1939, and 18th-
century street. Playground in the
garden. Workshops. Free.
Open: Tuesday to Saturday
10:00A.M. to 5:00P.M., Sunday 2:00
to 5:00P.M. Open Bank Holidays.
Tube: Liverpool Street then bus

♦
HAMLEYS
188–196 Regent Street, W1
Enormous toyshop with six floors
devoted to everything you can
possibly imagine from dolls and
teddy bears to trains and
computers. Soda Bar.
Tube: Oxford Circus

♦
LONDON TOY AND MODEL MUSEUM
21 Craven Hill, W2
A charming small museum with
over 3,000 toys and models
dating from the 18th century to
the present day (but no
touching). Trains, boats, planes
and a steam train and playbus in
the garden. Special events.
Open: Tuesday to Saturday
10:00A.M. to 5:30P.M., Sunday from
11:00A.M.
Tube: Lancaster Gate,
Paddington, Queensway

♦♦♦
LONDON ZOO
Regent's Park, NW1
The Discover Centre offers an
'animal experience', where
children can put on a helmet and
see how a housefly views the
world, or use a computer game
to 'run like a leopard'. Also
animal encounters, shows and
chats to keepers. Summer

Arklight laser shows with floats
on the canal. There are plans to
spend around £10 million on
expansion within the next few
years.
Open: 9:00A.M. to 6:00P.M. (7:00P.M.
Sundays) summer, 9:00A.M. to
4:00P.M. or dusk winter
Tube: Regent's Park, Camden
Town

♦
POLLOCK'S TOY MUSEUM
1 Scala Street, W1 (annexe
opposite and entrance in
Whitfield Street)
Two tiny houses with pint-sized
rooms and narrow staircases.
Founded by the man who made
Victorian toy theatres (which you
can buy along with toys in the
adjoining shop and also in the
theatre shop in Covent Garden).
Suitable for small adults and
children.
Open: Monday to Saturday
10:00A.M. to 5:00P.M.
Tube: Goodge Street

♦
TOBACCO DOCK
The Highway, E1
Huge new shopping and
restaurant complex converted
out of a 19th-century warehouse
in Docklands. Two replica
sailing ships to explore. One is a
Museum of Piracy through the
Ages, the other, the *Sky Lark*
schooner, a children's adventure
ship themed to Robert Louis
Stevenson's *Treasure Island*
complete with parrots. Charge
for ships.
Transport: Wapping or Shadwell
Underground; or Docklands Light
Railway to Shadwell from Tower
Gateway (Bank after summer
1991.) Then 5-minute (signposted) walk.

CHILDREN

Where to Eat

On the whole London restaurants do not take kindly to small children. Some even ban them altogether. You can't take under 14's into a pub unless it has a separate dining area. Restaurants that do cater well to families include:

Benihana, 100 Avenue Road, Swiss Cottage, NW3 (tel: 071 586 9508). A Japanese/American restaurant on the ground floor of a modern red and cream building opposite the station. The first in Britain of a USA chain offering 'performing' Japanese chefs (juggling pepper mills) on tables for eight, each with its own Hibachi grill. On weekend lunchtimes they have a cheap menu for under 10's (all food grilled in front of them), plus crayons and a Punch and Judy show (Sundays) in the bar. Not so cheap for grown-ups.

Chicago Meat Packers, 96 Charing Cross Road, WC2 (tel: 071 379 3277). Very cheap children's menu until 8:00 P.M. every day. On Sundays (noon to 4:00 P.M.) magicians work the tables. Crayons and cartoons in the bar area. Model railway.

Smollensky's Balloon, 1 Dover Street, W1 (tel: 071 491 1199). Opposite the Ritz. Noisy

Smollensky's Balloon is one of the places that welcomes children

basement, with weekend lunchtime attractions that include balloons, children's menus, a resident clown and a magician, plus videos, story time and Punch and Judy upstairs. Food is mostly steaks cooked on an open grill.

Entertainment

Barbican Centre, Silk Street, EC2 (tel: 071 638 4141). Changing exhibitions, stories, workshops, concerts (free) and Saturday and holiday cinema club.
Tube: Moorgate, Barbican
Half Moon Theatre, 213 Mile End Road, E1 (tel: 071 790 4000). Saturday morning shows for young children.

Tube: Stepney Green
ICA Children's Cinema, Nash House, The Mall, SW1 (tel: 071 930 0493) Regular Saturday and holiday film shows.
Tube: Charing Cross, Piccadilly Circus
The Little Angel Marionette Theatre, 14 Dagmar Passage off Cross Street, N1 (tel: 071 226 1787). Weekend and holiday puppet shows.
Tube: Highbury and Islington
National Film Theatre, South Bank, Waterloo, SE1 (tel: 071 928 3232). Weekend matinées of films. Also arts workshops at the National Theatre, Royal Festival Hall and Hayward Gallery (tel: 071 921 0848).
Tube: Waterloo
Polka Children's Theatre, 240 The Broadway, Wimbledon, SW19 (tel: 081 543 4888). Some way from central London but one of the best children's theatres in the capital with regular plays for all ages and also workshops. Puppets and playground. Closed Sundays and Mondays.
Tube: Wimbledon, South Wimbledon
Puppet Theatre Barge, Little Venice, Blomfield Road, W9 (tel: 071 249 6876). An interesting string puppet show on a moored Thames barge in Maida Vale, north London.
Tube: Warwick Avenue
Unicorn Theatre for Children, 6 Great Newport Street, WC2 (tel: 071 836 3334). The only solely professional children's theatre in the West End. Plays for all ages.
Performances: 1:30P.M. Tuesday to Friday, 2:30P.M. weekends and during school vacations.
Tube: Leicester Square

TIGHT BUDGET

Accommodation
● The Youth Hostels Association, 14 Southampton Street, WC2, near Covent Garden (tel: 071 240 3158) will help you find cheap accommodation.
● As an alternative, the London Tourist Board will direct you to bed and breakfast hotels.

Eating and Drinking
● Pubs with decent food are generally a lot cheaper than restaurants of whatever sort.
● Wine bars have reasonably priced food but the wine's expensive.
● The cheapest meals of all are to be found in cafés (sausage, bacon and egg, washed down by a cup of tea).
● You can get a cheapish meal at any number of restaurants serving pizzas.
● Indian and Chinese restaurants can also be cheap provided you steer clear of the new wave of 'designer' restaurants in and around Soho and Covent Garden.
● A cheap alternative to lunch is to buy a sandwich from any one of numerous sandwich bars.
● If you are prepared to start your evening off early, you can get half-price cocktails at bars that offer a Happy Hour.

Entertainment
● If you can't afford a full-price ticket to a West End theatre, go to the SWET ticket booth in Leicester Square for half-price tickets for that day.
● Cheaper still are the tickets for pub theatres or fringe theatres.
● Seats for the National Theatre are cheaper than for West End theatres.
● Free concerts are held in the National Theatre foyer, at the Barbican, in churches and in the piazza at Covent Garden.
● Several of London's museums are free, including the British Museum, though most expect some sort of donation (see What to See section).
● Some museums and galleries offer a discount if you have a student ID card.

St James's Park is free entertainment

DIRECTORY

Airports

Useful phone numbers:
Gatwick Flight Enquiries, tel: 0293 31299
Heathrow
Terminal 1, tel: 081 745 7720/4
Terminal 2, tel: 081 745 7115/6/7
Terminal 3, tel: 081 745 7413/4
Terminal 4, tel: 081 745 4540
London City Airport, tel: 071 474 5555
Luton Airport, tel: 0582 405100
Stansted Airport, tel: 0279 502520

Gatwick. To the south. Regular British Rail trains (every 15 mins, or hourly before 6:20A.M.) leave from within the terminal and run into Victoria Station in 35–45 mins.

Heathrow. To the west. You can get to and from central London by Underground, Airbus or taxi (very expensive).

The **Airbus** runs from all four Terminals to Victoria or Euston, stopping at several points including major hotel areas *en route*. The journey takes between 50 and 85 mins, with services every 20 or 30 minutes. Airbuses are equipped with wheelchair lifts and secure accommodation. At Victoria and Euston there are Carelink wheelchair-accessible bus services linking most of the central London main-line railway stations. You buy tickets (reasonably cheap) on the bus. Unless you are staying right in the centre of London this is the most relaxing bet, especially if you have heavy luggage, although it takes a bit longer than the tube, especially if traffic is heavy.

The Piccadilly **Underground** line runs from Terminals 1, 2 and 3 with a separate stop for Terminal 4. Trains run every 4–7½ minutes. Allow about 40 minutes to Piccadilly Circus, where you can change tube lines. If you've got heavy luggage you will have to struggle up stairs and escalators, and this can be an unpleasant experience!

A Night Bus service between Heathrow and Trafalgar Square (Route N97) operates nightly at about hourly intervals. Tickets bought on board.

You can buy **Heathrow Transfer Tickets** in advance through overseas travel agents or in London hotels, Travel Information Centres and travel agents.

London City Airport. Poor public transport, but a fleet of taxis is likely to be on hand at the tiny airport in Docklands. The Green Line 787 service runs from Victoria Station to the airport or trains run to Silvertown British Rail Station (less than a quarter of a mile from the airport) via West Ham or Stratford on the Underground. The River Bus (tel: 071 512 0555) provides a high speed catamaran service to Charing Cross Pier departures at half past the hour.

Luton. British Rail has a combined rail and coach link between St Pancras and the airport via Luton Station. The journey takes about 45 mins. Trains from King's Cross Thameslink are more frequent.

Stansted. Regular train service between Bishop's Stortford and Liverpool Street Station (takes 45 mins). Taxis and buses run between the station and airport. A direct rail link with Liverpool Street is expected to open during 1991.

UNDERGROUND

UNDERGROUND

- ○ Interchange stations
- ⇌ Connections with British Rail
- ⇌ Connections within walking distance
- ★ Closed Sundays
- ✳ Closed Saturdays and Sundays
- † See poster maps at Underground stations for opening and closing times of these stations

©Copyright London Regional Transport

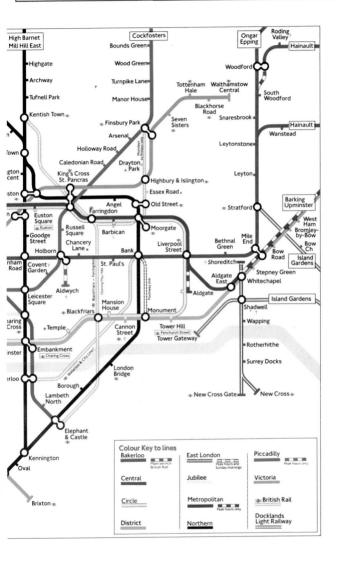

DIRECTORY

Camping

Sites include:

Eastway Cycle Circuit, Temple Mills Lane, E15 (tel: 081 534 6085). 4 miles (6.5km) from the city centre. Open March to October.

Hackney Camping, Millfields Road, E5 (tel: 081 985 7656). 4 miles (6.5km) from the centre. Open June to August.

Picketts Lock Centre, Picketts Lock Lane, N9 (tel: 081 803 4756). Open all year. 10 miles (16km) from the centre. Also campers.

Car Breakdown

If you are not a member of a

Car clamping is very effective – and very annoying

motoring organisation you can join on the spot.

The AA is Britain's largest motoring organisation, for breakdown assistance, 'phone 0800 887766 (free call service).

Car De-clamping

Hyde Park Police Car Pound, NCP parking lot, Park Lane, W1, is where to go if your car has been clamped (booted) in central London. After paying a fine you have to wait to get it released. Alternatively, the Car Clamp Recovery Club (tel: 071 235 9901) will, for a fee, do it for you. So will Clamp Rescue (tel: (071 837 7342).

Car Rental

Agencies include:

AA Car Hire, tel: 071 262 2223

Avis Rent A Car, tel: 081 848 8765

Central Rent A Car, tel: 071 730 6391

Continental City, tel: 081 968 3388

Guy Salmon Rentals, tel: 071 408 1255

Hertz Rent-A-Car, tel: 081 697 1799

International Car Rental, tel: 071 727 1467

Chauffeur-driven Cars

Brunswick Chauffeur Group, tel: 071 727 2611

Executive Car Hire (Maida Vale) Ltd, tel: 071 625 4252

Knightsbridge Car Service, tel: 071 261 1422

Magnum Chauffeur Drive, tel: 081 994 9123

Mayfair Chauffeur Hire, tel: (071 724 8432

Crime

It is best not to travel alone on the Underground at night. Keep bags and wallets safe, especially in crowded places. Otherwise London is much the same as other capitals.

Domestic Travel
By Car

Driving. Londoners are not bad drivers. One-way streets and trying to park legally are the main problems. There are special 'bus and taxi only' lanes that operate during peak hours in the West End and yellow 'boxes' in which you're not supposed to stop across junctions. Traffic in central London tends to snarl up during the 'rush hours' from 8:00A.M. to 10:00A.M. and from 5.00P.M. to 7:00P.M., with an additional jam after theatres close at around 10:30P.M. Seat belts are compulsory.

Parking. 'Car parks' (numerous National Car Park, NCP, parks) cost a little more than meters but at least you don't run the risk of overshooting your time and being 'clamped'. Two-hour meters are grey, 4-hour meters green. They all seem to gobble up coins (10p, 20p, 50p and £1). You are not allowed to 'feed' your meter when it has run out of time, but can use time already clocked up. Parking in some areas is free after lunchtime on Saturdays and all meters are free on Sundays. Traffic wardens are dressed in yellow and black; do not expect them to show you any mercy! You are not allowed to park in a resident's parking bay (unless you've got a permit), on a double yellow line (at any time) or on a single yellow line during working hours (usually including Saturday). Always check the little signs on lamp-posts to see

exactly what the rules are. An illegally parked car may get clamped or towed away to a Police Pound and you have to pay a fine to get it back (see **Car De-clamping**). If you can't find your car, ask a policeman.

Gasoline. Most 'petrol' stations are self-service and some stay open 24 hours a day. Unlike some of their counterparts in the US you cannot expect your windshield to be washed. If you need assistance you have to call the breakdown services (see **Car Breakdown**) or visit a garage with a mechanic. Most of these shut on weekends.

Public Transport

Buses. From the upper deck of one of London's double-decker buses there's often a good view of the capital. Three million passengers a day use the buses. Bus stops show bus numbers and timetables, but make sure you ring the bell or put your hand out at a 'red request' stop. There are 41 miles (66km) of bus lanes in central London, so while the rest of the traffic stands still, buses (and taxis) move freely. 'Pay-as-you-enter' night buses all stop at Trafalgar Square.

Coaches. Victoria Coach Station is the main London terminal for longer distance express coaches. Information from National Express Coaches (tel: 071 730 0202). London Transport runs coach tours in and around London and to places of interest nearby, with a courtesy pick up service from hotels. Most leave from Wilton Road Coach Station, near Victoria Station (tel: 071 227 3456). See also **Tours**.

Green Line coaches connect

central London with the suburbs. The main terminal is at Eccleston Bridge, near Victoria Station (tel: 081 668 7261).

Disabled. London Regional Transport runs a special unit to help disabled passengers, including braille maps for the visually impaired. There is a Dial-a-Ride minibus service and a Taxi-card plan (tel: 071 483 2519) which enables disabled people to use taxis at reduced cost. Airbus services between Heathrow and central London have been converted to accept wheelchairs. At Victoria and Euston the Carelink wheelchair-accessible bus service links main-line stations. There are also Mobility Buses with wheelchair access on routes in and around London, and the Docklands Light Railway can accommodate wheelchairs. Details from London Regional Transport, 55 Broadway, SW1 (tel: 071 227 3312).

Docklands Light Railway (DLR). The Docklands Light Railway, built to cater to the redevelopment of the Docklands, opened in 1987. An extension from Shadwell to Bank is due for completion in summer 1991. Until then the toy-town-like, blue and red, driverless trains run on weekdays only (until 9:30P.M.), departing from Shadwell or Tower Gateway and travelling via the Isle of Dogs to Island Gardens. Trains also run between Island Gardens and Stratford connecting with the Underground and British Rail. There are plans to extend eastwards to Beckton and the Royal Docks (December 1992) but no plans to connect the DLR

Familiar red buses in Oxford Street, outside Selfridges department store

to the London City Airport.

Information. British Rail Travel Centres (for personal visitors) are at: 14 Kingsgate Parade, Victoria Street, SW1; 407 Oxford Street, W1; and 87 King William Street, EC4. Telephone enquiries: 071 928 5100 (24-hour service).

Docklands Light Railway (tel: 071 222 1234).

London Transport 24-hour telephone information buses and Underground (tel: 071 222 1234). Recorded details on how services are running (tel: 071 222 1200).

London Regional Transport, 55 Broadway, SW1H 0BD (tel: 071 222 1234).

London Transport (LT) Information centres can be found at the following stations: Piccadilly Circus, Oxford Circus, King's Cross, Euston, Victoria and at Heathrow Central at Terminals 1, 2 and 3, and in all the arrival halls. They also sell tickets for excursions.

Minicabs. Minicabs cannot (at the time of writing) be hailed in the street. You have to telephone a central reservation number (see Yellow Pages).

Drivers use their own private cars. Ask about the price before you set off. There are plans to license them in the same way as taxis.

DIRECTORY

River Boats. RiverBus (tel: 071 512 0555) run regular commuter services (weekday only) along the river using high-speed, 62-seater airline-style catamarans. They run from Chelsea Harbour to the City, and from Charing Cross to Greenwich or the London City Airport, at 20-minute intervals. Stops (piers) *en route* are: Festival (by the South Bank Centre), Swan Lane (by London Bridge), London Bridge City (by Hays Galleria), and West India Dock (the Docklands).

Taxis. London taxicabs are black or maroon with a white licence plate on the back. You can hail them when the yellow taxi sign on the roof is alight. There are stands outside main-line stations and major hotels. A taxi can be ordered by telephoning 071 286 0286, 071 253 5000 or 071 272 0272/3030. A tip of between 10 and 15 per cent is expected. Taxi drivers are a gold mine of

Chelsea Harbour, base for a waterborne commuter service

information. The driver must use his meter (within the Metropolitan District). There is a minimum charge which shows on the clock, and supplements for luggage, after 8:00P.M. and on weekends.

Tickets. The **Visitor Travelcard** is available to overseas visitors, for 1, 3, 4 or 7 days and must be bought abroad. It offers virtually unlimited travel on the tube and buses (as well as discount vouchers to top attractions) and saves money on the regular Travelcard available once you get here. It can be bought from travel agents and London Transport sales agents abroad (you don't need a photo).

Heathrow Transfer Tickets (see **Airports**, page 107).

The regular **Travelcards** are available from any Underground station. They give freedom to travel on the buses or Underground for 1 or 7 days, or a month, within selected zones. You need a passport-sized photo for a 7-day or monthly card. Journeys for one-day cards have to start after 9:30A.M. (Monday to Friday) but you can travel any time on weekends. You can also get a bus pass (for a day, week or month) though they are not available for the central London zone.

Underground or tube tickets
Single or round-trip tickets must be bought at the station before you begin your journey either from a booth or from a machine. They must be kept to show an inspector who might board the train, and be handed in at the other end. If you leave a station before you get to your destination you have to buy a new ticket.

On **buses** you pay the conductor if there is one or the driver (as you board) if there isn't. Keep your ticket until you leave the bus in case an inspector gets on. London is divided up into six **zones** for fare purposes. Travel within central London is one zone. See maps at stations for details.

Children under 5 travel free. Under 14's get reduced rates (up to a third off the price), while 14 and 15-year-olds must carry a child-rate photocard (available from post offices and travel information centres with a photo and proof of age) for their reduction.

Trains. British Rail trains terminate in central London at various stations. Each station serves a network of stations in certain directions, as indicated below.

Moorgate, King's Cross (Yorkshire, North East and East Coast to Scotland). Tel: 071 278 2477

Euston, St Pancras (Midlands, North Wales, North West and West Coast to Scotland). Tel: 071 387 7070.

Paddington, Marylebone (West of England and South Wales). Tel: 071 262 6767.

Blackfriars, Cannon Street, Charing Cross, Fenchurch Street, Holborn Viaduct, Liverpool Street, London Bridge, Victoria and Waterloo (East Anglia and Essex, South East and South). Tel: 071 928 5100

Subway. The London Underground (or Tube) runs deep under the capital. Two and a half million people travel on it daily. There are 273 stations; those in central London are within a few minutes walk of each other. You shouldn't have to

The tube stations are gradually being re-vamped. Usually, they are safe and relatively clean

wait more than a few minutes for a train, but they can get uncomfortably crowded during the rush hour (roughly between 8:00 A.M. and 9:30 A.M. in the morning and 5:00 P.M. and 6:30 P.M. in the evening).

The Underground is divided into lines: Bakerloo, Central, Circle, District, East London, Jubilee, Metropolitan, Northern (which has one of the longest continuous railway tunnels in the world), Piccadilly and Victoria. Maps are easy to follow with each line having a different colour (see pages 108–9). The lines criss-cross each other making it easy to switch from one line to another although at some stations this can mean long walks on (well-lit) corridors or several rides down escalators. Some stations have numerous platforms, Baker Street has ten. The destination will be marked on the front of the train

and also on a board above the platform. Some lines branch into two so check the destination carefully. Most stations now have automatic barriers which open when you insert your ticket. All the main-line stations have connections with the Underground.

It is not permitted to smoke anywhere on the Underground. The Underground shuts at night with last trains leaving central London stations at midnight or soon after (an hour earlier on Sundays). First trains at 5:30A.M. (7:00A.M. on Sunday).

Electricity
240 volt, 50 cycle AC. Shavers operate on 240 or 110 volts. Plugs are three-prong. Adaptors are needed for US appliances.

Embassies/Consulates
Virtually every country is represented. Addresses are listed in the Yellow Pages phone book under 'embassies', or ask at the London Tourist Board.

Emergency Telephone Number
Dial 999 from any telephone, give the location, and state whether you want Fire, Police or Ambulance.

Entertainment (see page 89).
For what's going on, see weekly events listings in *Time out* or in the *Sunday Times* magazine.

Guidebooks
There are hundreds of books on London; a few of the most useful are listed below.

For General Information and Sightseeing:
AA London Guide
Blue Guide London (Black, Norton)
Britain Quick Guide to London (BTA)
The London Guide (and other titles – Nicholson)
London for Visitors (Time Out)
Michelin (Green) Tourist Guide London

For Art:
London Art and Artists Guide (Art Guide Publications/Black)

For Food and Drink:
Eating Out in London (Time Out)
Egon Ronay's Cellnet Guide
Good Food Guide (Consumers' Association/Hodder & Stoughton)

DIRECTORY

Good Pub Guide (Consumers' Association/Hodder & Stoughton)

For Shopping:
Directory of London's Shops and Services (Time Out)

For Students and Children:
London for Kids Magazine (Capital Radio)
London Student Guide (Time Out)

Hospitals
There are **24-hour casualty departments** at:
University College Hospital, WC1 (tel: 081 387 9300)
Guy's Hospital, SE1 (tel: 071 407 7600)
St Bartholomew's Hospital, EC1 (tel: 071 601 8888)
Moorfields Eye Hospital is situated at City Road, EC1 (tel: 071 251 0017)
Private emergency treatment is available from Medical Express, Chapel Place, W1 (tel: 071 499 1991)

Lost Property
Go to the nearest police station to report any loss.
If you have left something on a bus or tube the London Transport Lost Property Office (tel: 071 486 2496) is at 200 Baker Street, NW1 (open 9:30A.M. to 2:00P.M. Monday to Friday). For losses on trains ring up the arrival/departure point of the train you were travelling on. If you've left something in a taxi try to remember its licence number (not numberplate) and telephone 071 833 0996.

Money Matters
Banks: (See **Opening Times**) The terminals at Gatwick and Heathrow have 24-hour banks.

Currency: When banks are shut you can change money at major travel agencies like Thomas Cook, in the exchange offices at major department stores or in the numerous *bureaux de change* in high streets and at stations. Look for agencies that indicate they they follow the BTA Code of Conduct if you don't want to be cheated. There are exchange facilities at National Girobanks at some large post offices in central London.
VAT (Value Added Tax) is added to most goods and services at a standard rate of 17½ per cent. You can get relief from VAT on goods (*eg* shopping) but not services (*eg* restaurants) if you are a visitor from abroad. You may have to buy a minimum amount (usually over £100). Go to the information desk in the store in which you are shopping.

Opening Times
Banks. Monday to Friday 9:30A.M. to 3:30P.M. (3:00P.M. in the City). Also Saturday mornings (9:30A.M. to noon) at some branches.
Business. Normal business hours are 9:00 or 10:00A.M. to 5:30 or 6:00P.M. Offices are shut on weekends.
Museums and Galleries. Most are shut Christmas Day, Boxing Day (26 December) and New Year's Day, others on all public holidays and on Sunday mornings. Some museums and galleries are open shorter hours during the winter months.
Pubs. They are allowed to open from 11:00A.M. to 11:00P.M. Monday to Saturday and from noon to 3:00P.M. and again from 7:00P.M. to 10:30P.M. on Sundays. Not all open in the afternoon.

Many London pubs now stay open all day long

Shops. Most shops open at 9:00 or 9:30A.M. and shut at 5:30P.M. Shops open until 7:00P.M. or 8:00P.M. on Thursdays in the West End and on Wednesdays in Knightsbridge and Chelsea. They are open late daily in Covent Garden and Tobacco Dock. Some shops (the law is under review) are open on Sundays.

Pharmacies

There are pharmacies all over London. Bliss, 5 Marble Arch, W1, and Boots, 75 Queensway, W2 and 44 Piccadilly Circus, W1, are pharmacies which open late.

Places of Worship

Practically every religion is represented somewhere in London. See Places of Worship, etc, in Yellow Pages telephone directory.

DIRECTORY

Public Holidays

New Year's Day, Good Friday, Easter Monday, May Day (first Monday in May), Spring Bank Holiday (last Monday in May), Late Summer Holiday (last Monday in August), Christmas Day, Boxing Day (26 December).

Restrooms

There are some sanitised booths in the centre of London, otherwise there are public restrooms in main-line stations (both charge 10p) and most large stores. Parks have restrooms, and so do many squares.

Senior Citizens

Senior Citizens can get discounted entry into museums and galleries. There are also discounts for women over 60 and men over 65 on public transport on production of a Senior Citizen Railcard (UK residents), or a Rail Europe Senior Card or a BritRail Pass (overseas visitors).

Sports

Sportsline (tel: 071 222 8000) provides information on what's on where, whether you want to join in or just watch. The *Time Out Guide to Sport, Health and Fitness in London* from bookshops and newsagents lists venues. For the major sporting events like Ascot, Wimbledon or Henley you will need to book tickets well in advance through a ticket agency such as Keith Prowse (tel: 081 741 8999).

Students

London can seem like a pretty cruel city if you're a student. Essential reading is *Time Out's* free *Student Guide*, produced in conjunction with the NUS (National Union of Students), particularly if you are planning to stay for a while. Hang around the NUS in Malet Street, WC1, and you'll soon meet fellow students. An International Student ID Card is essential if you want discounts in museums, galleries, theatres, cinemas and public transport.

Westminster Abbey is one of the great treasures of London

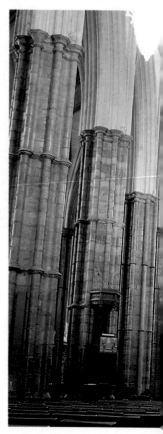

The main student organisations in London are Student Travel Association, 74 and 86 Old Brompton Road SW7 (tel: 071 937 9962, International; or 9921, European).
University of London Union, Malet Street, WC1 (tel: 071 580 9551). See also **Tight Budget**.

Telephones and Postal Services
Post Offices generally open 9:00A.M. to 5:30P.M. Monday to Friday; 9:00A.M. to noon on Saturdays. The post office behind Trafalgar Square in King William IV Street, WC2, is open from 8:00A.M. to 8:00P.M. Monday to Saturday. Stamps (only of certain values) are also available from machines outside some post offices, or as books of stamps in newsagents etc. The old red phone boxes have now almost all been replaced by open glass

DIRECTORY

booths. You can use a phonecard in some of them (available from post offices or newsagents). If you are out of cash call the operator (dial 100) to reverse charges/call collect. For calls within London, you need only use the prefix 071 (inner London), or 081 (outer London) if calling across the 071/081 boundary (check the number of the telephone you are calling on), otherwise simply dial the number. International numbers start with 010.

Push-button phones take coins which you insert after you have lifted the receiver but before you dial.

Useful numbers include:
Directory Enquiries (London) 142
Directory Enquiries (UK) 192
International Directory Enquiries 153
International Call Collect 155
Emergency 999

Ticket Agencies

Most agencies charge for their services on top of the price of tickets. They take credit card bookings over the phone. They include: First Call, tel: 071 240 7200
Ticketmaster, tel: 071 379 3295

Time

Greenwich Mean Time (GMT) is 5 hours ahead of US EST. British Summer Time (BST) begins in March when the clocks are put forward one hour. In October the clocks go back an hour to GMT. The official date is announced in the daily newspapers.

Tipping

Taxi drivers expect 10 to 15 per cent of the fare. Most restaurants include service in their bill. Some ethnic restaurants do not include service. Doormen at hotels expect 50p plus for getting taxis etc. Porters at railway stations expect £1. It is customary to tip sightseeing guides.

Tourist Offices

For information on what to do and see, events, entertainment, maps and hotel reservations:
The **British Travel Centre**, 12 Regent Street, SW1. Open weekdays 9:00A.M. to 6:30P.M. and 10:00A.M. to 4:00P.M. Saturdays and Sundays. Extended Saturday opening in summer. Tel: 071 730 3400 from 9:00A.M. to 6:30P.M. Monday to Friday, 10:00A.M. to 4:00P.M. Saturday (extended in Summer). Also American Express Travel Agency.
The **London Tourist Board** has **Information Centres** at:
Victoria Station Forecourt, SW1. Open Easter to end of October daily 8:00A.M. to 8:00P.M., and from November to Easter, Monday to Saturday 9:00A.M. to 7:00P.M., Sunday 9:00A.M. to 5:00P.M.
Harrods, Brompton Road, SW1 (Basement Booking Hall). Open store hours. Selfridges, Oxford Street, W1 (Basement). Open store hours. Tower of London, West Gate, EC3. Open Easter to end of October 9:30A.M. to 6:00P.M. (Sundays from 10:00A.M.)
Heathrow Terminals 1, 2, 3 Underground Station Concourse. Open daily 8:00A.M. to 6:30P.M. Liverpool Street Station. Open Monday to Saturday 9:00A.M. to 6:30P.M., Sunday 8:30A.M. to 3:30P.M.
The **London Tourist Board** number is 071 730 3488. Monday to Saturday 9:00A.M. to 6:00P.M.

Part of Buckingham Palace's Changing of the Guard – a 'must' for many visitors

For travel outside London:

Northern Ireland Tourist Board, tel: 071 493 0601

Scottish Tourist Board, tel: 071 930 8661

Wales Tourist Board, tel: 071 409 0969

There are also regional tourist offices throughout Britain.

Tours of London

If you want a guided tour of the capital there are numerous possibilities.

By Boat. The Regent's Canal runs from Camden Lock to the Zoo and Little Venice (Maida Vale): a quiet backwater with a towpath you can walk along. Companies include:

Jason's Trips (tel: 071 286 3428). They use gaily painted narrow boats and trips last 1½ hours. Easter to early October. Refreshments and commentary on board. Also lunch and dinner cruises. Boats leave from Little Venice and Camden Lock.

Jenny Wren Cruises (tel: 071 485 4433). Leave from Camden Lock. They are based at 250 Camden High Street on the bridge over the canal. Sunday lunchtime cruises run all year.

London Waterbus Company (tel: 071 482 2550). Runs daily on the hour from Camden Lock to Little Venice from April to September (weekends only rest of year, every 90 minutes). The company also run day-long trips through East London to Limehouse and the Docklands.

The Thames. Covered cruise boats ply the river. Most boats have snack bars on board with informal commentaries (in English only). They depart regularly from the following piers:

Richmond (tel: 081 892 1741) to Hampton Court and a circular cruise to Teddington Lock.

Westminster down river (tel: 071 930 4721/2062) to the Tower, the Thames Barrier and Greenwich (all year); up river to Kew, Richmond and Hampton Court (summer only). Also circular cruises and evening and lunch cruises.

Charing Cross (tel: 071 839 3572) to the Tower and Greenwich; also evening cruises.

Tower (tel: 071 488 0344) up river to Westminster and down river to Butler's Wharf and Greenwich (all year) with a ferry to see HMS *Belfast*.

Greenwich (tel: 081 858 0079) to Tower, Charing Cross, Westminster and down river to the Thames Barrier. Also lunch cruises every Sunday.

General riverboat information (tel: 071 730 4812).

By Bus. London Transport run 1½ hour sightseeing tours by double-decker bus (open-topped in summer), with a commentary by a qualified guide. They start from Marble Arch, Victoria, Piccadilly and Baker Street, and French and German speaking guides are also available. There are sightseeing buses to the Zoo (between March and early September) from Oxford Circus and Baker Street stations.

By Coach. Numerous companies offer coach tours of London as well as excursions to nearby places of interest.

On Foot. Guided walks usually start at Underground stations. Some follow a theme – Cockney London, The Jewish East End and Jack the Ripper among them. Companies include:

Citisights (tel: 081 806 4325). Led by archaeologists and historians working with the City of London Archaeological Trust at the Museum of London, City Walks (tel: 071 937 4281).

Foreign language tours available:
Cockney London Walks (tel: 081 504 9159)
Literary tours of Hampstead village: Exciting Walks (tel: 071 624 9981), Footloose in London (tel: 071 435 0259).
Themed Walks: London Walks (tel: 081 441 8906). Hidden and unusual London Streets of London (tel: 081 882 3414)
Tours by Tape (with a guidebook, in several languages) are available from the Tourist Information Centre bookshop at Victoria Station.

One of the most relaxing ways to see London is to take a boat trip. The view below is looking upstream from Tower Bridge. The Chelsea Pensioner (right) spends his time at the Royal Hospital. The hospital was founded in 1682 for veteran and invalid soldiers

INDEX

ACKNOWLEDGEMENTS

The Automobile Association would like to thank the following photographers, libraries and hotels for their assistance in the compilation of this book.

AA PHOTO LIBRARY 82 S & O Mathews, 34 R Surman.

SUSAN GROSSMAN 36 Freud Museum, 88 Sandringham Hotel, 104/5 Smollensky's Balloon.

HALCYON HOTEL 86/7.

NATURE PHOTOGRAPHERS LTD 46 Red deer stag (C B Carver), 49 Ancient oaks (F V Blackburn), 50 Purple hairstreak, 52 Green sandpiper, 53 Yellow rattle, 55 Grazing marsh, 56/7 Epping Forest, 59 Water rail (P R Sterry).

RITZ HOTEL 64.

SPECTRUM COLOUR LIBRARY Cover

BARRY SMITH was commissioned to take all the remaining photographs, and these are now in the AA's Photo Library.

Author's Acknowledgement:
Susan Grossman thanks the London Tourist Board for their help in preparing this book.